T0129864

Rebuild Your
Spiritual Wall

Rebuild Your
Spiritual Wall

PASTOR LERONE DINNALL

REBUILD YOUR SPIRITUAL WALL

Scripture quotations from the Holy Bible, King James Version (Authorized Version). First published in 1611. Quoted from the KJV Classic Reference Bible.

iUniverse books may be ordered through booksellers or by contacting:

iUniverse
1663 Liberty Drive
Bloomington, IN 47403
www.iuniverse.com
1-800-Authors (1-800-288-4677)

ISBN: 978-1-5320-6802-7 (sc)
ISBN: 978-1-5320-6803-4 (e)

Print information available on the last page.

iUniverse rev. date: 03/25/2019

Contents

Tributes

"A Special Thanks to My Wife Taina Dinnall and our Family, without The Continual Encouragement and Support from My Family, I know that there would not be a Desire to Continue to Push and Evolve to The Continual Higher Level In God. I Thank My Wife for all those Prayers with Tears, Fastings with Clean Hands and A Pure Heart, that helps to Accelerate The Blessings and Favors of God upon our lives and that of The Ministry that God Gave us, Thank You".

"To My Spiritual Family, To All The Members of The Church of Jesus Christ Fellowship Savannah Cross Ltd. I Thank you for Believing with me, Thank you for Praying and Fasting with me, Thank you for Serving God in the Fashion that Will Force Growth. I Thank you for your Continual Prayers unto God for All My Success and The Success of this Ministry. I Thank you for placing your trust in this Ministry with The Leading of Almighty God, Thank you for allowing me to be A Servant of God, A Pastor and A Leader for The Church and the Young People who are The Future of This Ministry. I Thank The Church of Jesus Christ Fellowship Savannah Cross Ltd. Jamaica West Indies for Keeping and Maintaining The Sacrifice Clean, that there will be A Continual Acceptance from The Father Above".

"A Special Thank you towards the Management and Publishing Team of Iuniverse, that opened their Thoughts and Resources towards the idea and Possibilities of supporting This Ministry to allow The Word of God to reach The World. The Ministry of The Church of Jesus Christ Fellowship Savannah Cross Ltd. Say Thank you for Capturing our Vision and helping us to impact the lives of many that are to be Saved, that they too will be able to Impact the lives of others. Thank you Iuniverse, God's Richest Blessings".

Introduction

All Glory, Honor and Praise Be Unto Jesus Christ, The Lamb of God, The Only Unlimited Mind of The Universe; In Him Every Knees Must Bow and Every Tongue will Confess that He Is Lord.

I am Privileged, almost speechless of this opportunity to be in this Position another time to Introduce to The World The Mind of God to His People.

This Book with the Title Being Rebuild Your Spiritual Wall, is Book Number 2 from The Ministry of The Church of Jesus Christ Fellowship Savannah Cross Ltd. Jamaica West Indies. The Leader of The Church Is The Eternal Spirit of God Being Our Lord Jesus Christ; The Servant placed at this Location in Jamaica is yours truly Pastor Lerone Dinnall.

This Book with Title Rebuild Your Spiritual Wall is indeed a continuation from The First Book, known As: "God Steps In". It is found that whenever it was observed in The Bible that The Lord Renewed His Covenant with His People, there were always a set of Instructions Given, to thus ensure that Man will be able to now Rebuild The Relationship that they once had with The God of The Universe.

Therefore, It will be observed in the contents of this Book, that there will be Revealed, Anointed Instructions from The Spirit and Mind of God unto His People, to know Exactly what path to take for A Child of God who was once Broken, to now be able find their steps back into The Hands of The Potter, to Allow The God of Creation to

Remold, Rebuild, Fenced In and Grant Continual Protection for The Child that will now Abide In God's Will.

The Beginning of this Book will Introduce The Spiritual Food that every Child that is Destined for The Kingdom of God must be Born of this Appetite, in order to Create A New Diet to Entertain these Spiritual Activities within their lives, and also in the lives of their Generation. Thus it is seen that the first three Chapter of this Book will focus on Prayers and Fasting. Without these Spiritual Food, there is no Path for A Child of God to start the Journey to Rebuild A Meaningful Relationship with God. Man Shall Not Live By Bread Alone, But By Every Word That Proceeded Out Of The Mouth Of God. Deuteronomy 8:3.

It must be observed within our lives, What it was, and Who it was that brought forth a spirit to entertain a thought within our minds to think that we can survive without God. These spirits is in fact the other gods, of which their Main Focus is not to take The Place of God, because they can't; these spirits are rather focused on God's Children to Rob us of The Anointing, The Blessing and The Authority that God Has Imparted upon A Child of God to Have; which is, and always was to Lead, to Care for, and also to Build the old waste places of The Earth to direct those who are lost, to find their way back into The Hands of God. Therefore, Chapters four and five will ensure that The God Lead People are focused on The Manifestation of The Spirit of God rather than being swayed by the Glamour and Fashions of this World that will seek to allow us to forget about Our God that is always Current, to now hang our Salvation on a shelve for those things of The World that will and must past away.

Climbing The Spiritual Ladder of this Book, it is Observed that Tithing for any Child of God must be Carefully Understood Before Giving, because The Lord Said, My People Are Destroyed for a Lack of Knowledge. Through Divine Revelations from God, The Lord Revealed to me, so that I can Reveal to His People that Tithes Is Holy and the person that Gives Tithes, must Reflect The Likeness of Holy Characteristics from God, or else it is not Tithes, but Offerings.

Chapters Seven to Nine expresses the Importance of The Surroundings of A Child of God, to therefore allow for us to Identify that every person carries a specific type of Anointing within their Circle, therefore the Guarding of A Child of God Surroundings must be Treated with Great Value, to thus Protect that which God Has Given For His Children to Possess. Chapters Eight and Nine is also Seasoned with Special Prayers for The Continual Growth of A Child of God that is Seeking to abide Within The Will of Almighty God.

Making progress through this Book, it Must Be Understood that Church Is The Spiritual Home for every Child of God, it is The Classroom for Spiritual Training, and it is Identified by The Spirit of God that Moves to Create An Environment that His Children can Learn all that is Within The Mind of God In Measurement for A Child of God to Learn. Therefore, It Must be realized by Every Spirit Filled Child of God to Understand that If The Spiritual House, of which The Spirit of God Should Have Full Access to Move, If this House of God is being Affected with Influence of other gods, then we know through The Teachings of The Bible that The Spirit of The Living God Will No Longer Be Entertained within The House that was Designated to Occupy The Presence of God. These Three Chapters, Ten, Eleven and Twelve are geared towards opening the eyes of God's Children, to allow us to understand that if we are not Alert to Keep The House of God Being Special and Holy, then our Generation which will follow us, will bear the Consequences of Losing The Relationship with God.

There are many Sons of God that have not yet evolved to The Higher Level of Complete Trust In God; Yes, We go to Church; We Pray Often, We Fast and Read our Bibles; but to Acquire The Level of Spiritual Assurance is an Experience that not many of us have Attained. The Thirteen Chapter of this Book will bring each Child of God on a Journey of A Vision that The Lord Gave to me, to Allow Me to Understand that the spirit of Fear is A Continual Enemy to The Spirit and Will of God In The Life of any Child of God. The Lord Revealed in this Chapter that Fear is Developed and is being entertained within the Minds of His Children because we do not Understand that Fear Breeds and Births the spirits of Doubts and Confusions, which limits A Child shall not prevail against it. And I Will Give unto thee the Keys of The Kingdom of Heaven: and whatsoever thou shalt Bind on Earth Shall Be Bound In Heaven; and whatsoever thou shalt Loose on Earth Shall Be Loosed In Heaven".

The Eternal Spirit of God Goes before this Book, I Pray through The Access of The Holy Ghost that whoever comes in contact with this Book, that their lives and the lives of their Generation will Be Forever Changed to The Will and Glory of God's Kingdom.

To The Only Unlimited Mind of The Universe, Jesus Christ The Lamb of God, to Him Be All Glory, Honor and Praise, Be Blessed By God's Word, Amen.

Opening Scriptures

Nehemiah Chapter 1.

The words of Nehemiah the son of Hachaliah. And it came to pass in the month Chrisleu, in the twentieth year, as I was in Shushan the palace, That Hanani, one of my brethren, came, he and certain men of Judah; and I asked them concerning the Jews that had escaped, which were left of the captivity, and concerning Jerusalem. And they said unto me, The Remnant that are left of the captivity there in the province are in great affliction and reproach: the wall of Jerusalem also is broken down, and the gates thereof are burned with fire. And it came to pass, when I heard these words, that I sat down and wept, and mourned certain days, and Fasted, and Prayed before The God of Heaven, And Said, I Beseech Thee, O Lord God of Heaven, The Great and Terrible God, that Keepeth Covenant and Mercy for them that love Him and Observe His Commandments: Let Thine Ear now Be Attentive, and Thine Eyes Open, that Thou Mayest Hear the Prayer of Thy servant, which I Pray before Thee now, day and night, for the Children of Israel Thy Servants, and confess the sins of the children of Israel, which we have sinned against Thee: both I and my father's house have sinned.

We have dealt very corruptly against Thee, and have not kept The Commandments, nor The Statutes, nor The Judgements, which Thou Commandedst Thy Servant Moses. Remember, I beseech Thee, the word that thou Commandedst Thy Servant Moses, Saying, If ye transgress, I Will Scatter you abroad among the nations: But if ye Turn unto Me, and keep My Commandments, and Do Them; though there were of you cast out unto the uttermost part of Heaven, yet Will I Gather them from thence, and Will Bring them unto the place that I have Chosen to Set My Name there. Now These are Thy Servants and Thy People, whom Thou hast Redeemed by Thy Great Power, and by Thy Strong Hand. O Lord, I Beseech Thee, let now Thine Ear Be Attentive to the Prayer of Thy Servant, and to the Prayer of Thy Servants, who desire to fear Thy Name: and Prosper, I Pray Thee, Thy Servant this day, and Grant him Mercy in the sight of this man. For I was the king's Cupbearer.

2 Chronicles 29:1-11.

Hezekiah began to reign when he was five and twenty years old, and he reigned nine and twenty years in Jerusalem. And his mother's name was Abijah, the daughter of Zechariah. And he did that which was right in the Sight of The Lord, according to all that David his father had done. He in the first year of his reign, in the first month, opened the doors of The House of The Lord, and repaired them. And he brought in the Priests and the Levites, and gathered them together into the east street, And said unto them, Hear me, ye Levites, Sanctify now yourselves, and Sanctify The House of The Lord God of your fathers, and carry forth the filthiness out of The Holy Place. For our fathers have trespassed, and done that which was evil in The Eyes of The Lord our God, and have forsaken Him, and have turned away their faces from the habitation of The Lord, and turned their backs. Also they have shut up the doors of The Porch, and put out The Lamps, and have not burned Incense nor Offered burnt Offerings in The Holy Place unto The God of Israel. Wherefore The Wrath of The Lord was upon Judah and Jerusalem, and He Hath Delivered them to Trouble, to Astonishment, and to Hissing, as ye see with your eyes. For, lo, our fathers have fallen by the sword, and our sons and our daughters and our wives are in captivity for this. Now it is in mine heart to make A Covenant with The Lord God of Israel, that His Fierce Wrath may turn away from us. My sons, be not now negligent: for The Lord hath Chosen you to stand before Him, to Serve Him, and that ye should Minister unto Him, and burn Incense.

Mindset

Just A Small Instruction from The Mind of God Can Change People, Churches, Communities, Cities, Nations, Countries and even The World.

- The Mission of This Book is to Change Lives for The Glory of God's Kingdom.

- If We Are Indeed The Tithes of God, then We are going to Consider our Walk in this Life.

- God Can Be Found In All Nations, Languages and Cultures; We are all ONE In God's Eyes, there is no Black or White, Chinese, Canadians, Indians, African, Australians, Mexican, Europeans, English, Americans, Japanese, Russians Etc. But One People, coming into Agreement to Acknowledge that There Is Only One God That Controls The Entire World.

- Think for One Minute of The Future and The Inheritance Were Going to leave for Our Children if we make the Wrong Decisions in Life.

- Whenever The Children of Israel Sinned, it took many years for them to Escape from The Bondage of Sin, to find themselves back In The Will of God.

- Our Children Didn't Fail The Future, We Failed The Present for Our Children because We Did Not Stand for God. It's Our Freewill to Stand Up for God to thus make A Bright Future for Our Children.

- The Only Enemy We Have Is Sin.

- The Only Friend We Have Is God, and His Will Being Done and His People that have Align themselves to God's Will Being Done.

- Love God First, then The Love for Everything Else Will Be Automatic.

- It's Never Too Late For God to Make A Change.

- God Never Surrenders The Mission of Saving Grace, But Rather, We Gave up on God. Don't Give Up On God!

The Body Of Prayer

To God Be The Glory Great things He Has Done; so Loved He the World that He Gave us His Son. I Greet all My Father's Children in The Wonderful Name of Jesus Christ; I count it as a privilege to be writing another wonderful Message for The Children of God.

I know we've been receiving a lot of Messages lately concerning Prayer; and while there may be a lot of people that don't see Prayer as an important factor in their lives; we The People of God knows better, and we are well aware of the importance of Prayer and we are also knowledgeable of The Revelation that there is **No End to Prayer**. Just as it is an everyday routine for us to get up out of our beds in the morning and get ourselves cleaned for the day's activity; so is it with Prayer, everyday Prayer is necessary; every step we take it's important; every decision we try to make, Prayer is of great necessity for us to seek The Face of The Lord FIRST before we go ahead and do whatsoever we desire to do.

There was a King in The Bible by the name of David, The Bible Said that he was found to be a man after God's own Heart; The Bible also described the life of David as one of complete trust in God. The trust David had was so great that whatever David was about to do, he made it a duty to make sure that he Consulted The Face and Permission of God first, realizing that he could not accomplish anything unless God

Had Given The Approval. An example of one of these event can be found in The Book of 2 Samuel Chapter 5:17-25.

The Body of Prayer; this sounds a little strange; if you're not doing a study on Prayer, along with Revelations that only God Can Give, only this will allow for us to realize that there is more to Prayer than that which meets the eyes. While Prayer is important, it is also necessary for us to know that not all Prayer that is made is actually Answered, and this is a Fact that not many people would want to acknowledge.

Psalms 66:18. Says:

"If I regard iniquity in my heart, The Lord Will Not Hear me".

We should Identify by now that Prayer Is Special, we should also know that Prayer must have Special Ingredient in it to allow it to actually be called A Prayer. Many of the Prayers that are being offered is not really Prayer; in The Eyes of God, they are actually conversations of pride that we are having with ourselves; and it has not even started to have the necessary ingredience that it needs to actually allow it to be called A Prayer Offered to God. St Luke Chapter 18:9-14. Best describe this knowledge.

The Bible Declares in The Book of Malachi Chapter 1:8. Which States:

"And if ye offer the blind for Sacrifice, is it not evil? And if ye offer the lame and the sick, is it not evil? Offer it now unto thy Governor; will he be pleased with thee, or accept thy person? Saith The Lord of Host".

Some of the Prayers that we Offer to God, if we should really Investigate what is being Offered, we would have discovered that we are just like The Children of Israel, when they became Corrupt and Proud, looking at The Living God without the True Meaning of Who God Is, Which Is, and always will Be A Holy God Who Deserves and Requires Holy Sacrifice.

The Bible Declares in The Book of St Luke Chapter 11:1. That the Disciples when they both saw and heard Jesus Christ Prayed; they asked Him with great desire that He Would Teach them how to Pray. This passage of Scripture moves My Intelligence to ask a lot of questions. These are some of the questions that pops out of My Mind:

1. The request asked from the Disciples unto Jesus Christ: "Teach us how to pray". Was it that the Disciples of The Lord knew not how to Pray; it would seem next to impossible that Prayer has been around for centuries before Jesus Christ even came on the scene Physically.

2. Or was it that when they heard and saw the way in which Jesus Christ Prayed, it made them realize that, that which they called Prayer, there is a lot more to it than that which they understood. And because of the experience of seeing, hearing and observing the connection that took place because of how Real, Purposeful and filled with ingredient the Prayer was. Those Disciples realized something important; what they called Prayer, was not even scratching the surface of connecting with The Father of The Universe. And because it was not yet Prayer, they came to the conclusion and asked:

"Master Teach us How to Pray".

Jesus Christ Seeing their need of knowing how can a person truly offer unto God an Accepted Prayer; He Gave them an Example which is found in the same Book St Luke Chapter 11:1-4. Now looking on the Prayer and observing the details in the Message of The Prayer, we would actually realize what Jesus Christ actually Gave to them, was A Body of Prayer, for them to follow; and if they would only follow the fundamentals and the meaning of how this Prayer is to be offered to God, they would have actually meet all the Requirements to construct an Accepted Prayer before God that will have Meaning and Connection.

THE BODY OF PRAYER

Prayer Of Thanksgiving

Studies of The Bible and Revelations from God Shows that one of the most important part to The Body of Prayer is A Prayer of Thanksgiving; by doing this we will ensure that we have Acknowledge God for Who He Is; what He Has Done and for What He Is About To Do; also along with Giving Thanks, we have to make sure that we Give Him Praise; let God know that there is no one in the World that can be compared to Him.

Psalms 148-150. Can be read for Reference towards Giving God Thanks.

Prayer of Confession of Sins

After The Prayer of Thanksgiving it is important to now offer unto God A Prayer of Confession of sin; this is where we would confess all our sins before God. I know that in the example that The Lord Gave us, it has us asking God for what we want God to Do for us; But Studies have Revealed that confessing of our sin is of greater importance than that of doing A Prayer of Request. Reason being, if we don't confess our sins, that means that God's Ears Will Remain Closed concerning the Prayer that we are offering to Him; because sin is the only enemy that keeps us away from The Favors of God.

Now it is important for us to make sure that we confess all sins; even those sins that we know not about; the sin of the Mind; the sin of our Forefathers; the sin of our parents and sin of our children, another way to look on it, is that we are confessing the sins of The Past, The Present and for the Future. It is also important for us to make sure that we ask God to Help us to forgive others, because if we don't forgive, neither will God Forgive us. We have to make sure that we have Repented of all wrong doings.

Prayer of Request

After The Prayer of Confession, this will now create the pathway for us to go to the next Prayer, being A Prayer of Request. This Prayer will now have the assurance that whatever we ask God to Do for us, there is now an Open Door / Access; The Windows of Heaven Open to receive and more importantly, The Ears of God Almighty Receiving that which we have asked for.

Prayer of Brotherly Love

The fourth Prayer is A Prayer of Brotherly Love, this is the part of the Prayer that God Is Searching for, to See if, through all our Praying; if we are going to remember that one of The Main Commandment that God Gave is that we should love each other as we love ourselves. That which The Lord Is Seeking for in this Prayer, is to See if we are going to Pray for the success of others, as it is that we have Prayed for our personal success. Many a times we go into Prayer thinking that it's all about Me, Myself, and I; God Looks on this Attitude and Realize that we are selfish and full of Pride; and one of the main thing that God Hates is a person that is Proud.

Proverb 6:16-19.

"These six things doth The Lord Hate: yea, seven are an Abomination unto Him: A Proud look, a Lying tongue, and Hands that shed innocent blood, An Heart that deviseth wicked imagination, Feet that be swift in running to mischief, A False witness that speaketh lies, and he that Soweth discord among brethren".

Therefore, In this Prayer of Brotherly Love, we would Pray for a change in our Neighbour's life, that they will find God for themselves, Pray for their Wellbeing, Pray for their Growth, Pray for their Success. Allow me to Reveal a little secret that The Lord Has Shared with me; when we spend time Praying for others, we will now Accelerate our personal request that we have made to God to come through at an even quicker pace.

The song writer caught the vision, when he said I found the Answer, I learned how to Pray. I have now learned how to Pray, and also reminding myself that there is always room for improvements. Realizing this fact, I am now of this character, wherever a person is, and whosoever that person is, and whatever that person has done to me; I going to make sure that I'm the first person that is going to Pray for them, and My Prayer will be A Good Prayer, for all their benefits and success; and that they will have a long and meaningful life; I will also Pray that God will Forgive them for the wrongs they have done to me, and also ask God to Allow me to forgive them; because no one is going to stand in the way of My Prayers being Answered, so that I will be next in line to Receive My Blessing.

Prayer of Thanksgiving

The fifth Prayer is another Prayer of Thanksgiving unto God. The Lord Revealed to me that in this Prayer, that the same way we would start the Prayer, it is the same way the Prayer should end; we start off with Thanksgiving and Praise, we will now end with Thanksgiving and Praise unto The God of all gods and The King of all kings. I got this Revelation by A Visit from God, after I got Married and Gave My Groom's speech, I Gave to God All Praise for Allowing me to get Married. The Lord Told me in The Vision that I Did well in My Speech, but I must receive this Revelation to know that whenever I'm Giving to God Thanks and Praise, I must make certain that the same way I begin to Give God Thanks and Praise, is the same way I must end by Giving God Thanks and Praise.

These Prayers Offered to God, brings forth a completion of that which is called The Body of Prayer or The Accepted Prayer.

Now you may ask this Question: Why is this The Body of Prayer? Let me answer that question in this manner; The Bible Said in St John 4:24. That God Is A Spirit and they that Worship Him must Worship Him in Spirit and in Truth. Now let us examine what The Word of The

6

Lord Is Saying unto us; The Bible is Allowing us to know one of God's Main Character Secret concerning how we should Worship.

Two Main Points:

1. It must be done in Spirit for it to be Accepted.
2. It must be done in Truth for it to be considered as Worship.

Now after observing these facts, there is a Revelation I would like to express. The Spirit of God which is The Holy Ghost has Seven Characteristic which are known as The Seven Spirit of God, which is a combination of being One Spirit, which is The Holy Ghost. These Seven Function of The Spirit of God are essential, they are The Seven Abilities or Manifestations of God in its Fullest Measure. Now The Characters of this One Spirit in different Manifestation are as follows:

1. The Spirit of God that has the ability to MOVES through all things.
2. The Spirit of God that has the ability to SEES all things.
3. The Spirit of God that has the ability to FEELS all things.
4. The Spirit of God that has the ability to HEARS all things.
5. The Spirit of God that has the ability to SMELLS all things.
6. The Spirit of God that has the ability to TASTE all things.
7. The Spirit of God to UNDERSTAND and to have the KNOWLEDGE of all things thus to shows Complete WISDOM concerning all things. This Reflects The Full Operation and Manifestation of THE GOD HEAD.

All these Seven Spirit individually is actually what makes up The Ability of The Almighty God; and these Abilities are to be found in The Functions of The Holy Ghost.

Now you may ask yourself, what does this have to do with The Body of Prayer? It has everything to do with it. When we Pray, Teach, Worship, Praise, Fast and even Live; it is at that time that God Searches to See if that which we are actually doing is measured up to His Requirements to be done in Spirit and in Truth. God Puts each and every Sacrifice that we have made in a Scale to See if it is actually at the measurement that we say it is at. God Uses His Spirit to Search and to Find out the Truth.

Let's give an example: Let us say that I came to A Fasting Service, and for my benefit I made sure that I wear the right apparel, behave the way I'm supposed to behave, and even played a main part in the Fasting service and make people believe that I'm observing a Fast; but it turns out that I knew that this was just a show. Although I would have made a lot of effort to fool others and convince myself that I was on Fasting, there is The Spirit of God Present that first MOVES to LOOK, then FEELS, then LISTEN to HEAR, then SMELLS My Sacrifice, after that TASTE to UNDERSTAND that God May have The KNOWLEDGE to Preform Equity which means equal right by the full measure of WISDOM He Possess. Then after God Has Search and Found out that we do not measure up to His Requirements, then many days or months or years after we get to realize that we were actually wasting time in The Presence of God, because we have not receive any rewards nor Prayers being answered for our efforts; neither sin being forgiven for those many days of Fasting.

In regards to The Body of Prayer; we must consider carefully when we Pray, if that Prayer resembles the replica of that which is Given for Example by Jesus Christ.

Is it actually A Body of Prayer when we Pray!

Does our Prayer Meets all the requirement that is necessary to Receive an Answer from God.

In Revelations Chapter 5:8. The Bible Says that The Odours of The Prayer of the Saints goes up before God. Now look into that very Scripture that is mention; the Odour of the Prayer of the Saints. What I get to understand about this Scripture Is:

Odour according to The Bible Dictionary in this Scripture is known as incense, which means the smell of sweet fragrance to that of perfume; now for the Prayer of the Saints to be compared to that of perfume in the Nostrils of God, it therefore means that God Has Already Searched for Himself by The Holy Ghost to Discern among us what is truly The Body of Prayer which is offered in Spirit and in Truth.

Now if you think about it, the words Spirit and Truth is the Standard for God's Acceptance; these words represent A Special Key that God Has Given His People, the opportunity to acquire for them to have the access to open the door that leads towards receiving God's Full Attention to Hear and then to Answer. Many people are of the belief that it is the many years that we spend in Church that makes a person qualify to Receive of God or to Enter Heaven. We have got to start thinking different, it is not the quantity of the time spent in The House of The Lord or in His Presence, but it is true and it is a FACT according to this Message; it's only THE QUALITY of the time that we spend with God really matters.

I have made up My Mind that if I'm going to Church and I feel that I'm not able to Worship God in Spirit and in Truth, then it would be better for me to sit that day out, and get myself ready for the next Worship session, that I can come forth into God's Presence and be able to Worship Him in Spirit and in Truth. Because if I insist to be in God's Presence, and have not found myself to Be The Sacrifice to Offer Worship, I am fearful that I might develop an attitude of coming to Church and just being a person that is pretending or is just there to keep the bench warm.

God Is Seeking all over this World for Saints of God that are True Worshippers; I need you to ask yourself this Question:

"AM I A TRUE WORSHIPPER THAT WILL WORSHIP IN SPIRIT AND IN TRUTH"? _____.

To God Be The Glory, Great Things He Has Done; so Loved He the World that He Gave us His Son. May The Blessings of God Be upon you always; let us continue to Pray for each other's strength in God, In The Mighty Name of Jesus Christ. From the Servant of God, Your Friend, Brother and Fellow worker, Pastor Lerone Dinnall.

The Ingredient In Our Prayers Is What Makes It A Body Of Prayer When We Pray.

LORD, What Should I Ask You For When I Pray?

Message # 15   **Written in the year 2015.**

Give me You, everything else can wait; give me You, I hope I'm not too late. Greetings in The Wonderful Name of Jesus Christ The Only Living God. Receive I Pray this another Message Inspired and Directed through The Spirit of God.

Have we ever considered to ask The Lord, what is it that He would want us to ask of from Him! Think about it, we spend most of our time and energy in meaningless Prayers, asking for a whole lot of things that we will never receive, because if God is Truthful to us, as He Says He Is; then we must be aware that The Scriptures Says that God Will Never Be A Father to us and Know that, what we are asking for is indeed going to be A Stumbling Block, A Stone, A Serpent; or something that is going to cause Harm to us and our family. When we have fully come to the realization and the understanding; we will get to see for ourselves that God Is Basically Protecting us from what we think is right and good for ourselves.

Experience in life is good; many people try their very best to shy away from the experiences of life that will be used for the sole purpose to give us the Ingredient to make us to become the man that God Needs us to Become. And it is with our Experience and Responsibilities that we will know, what it is to be a Father or a Mother, and therefore we will now have the duty to ensure that our little child is protected from things that so easily attracts that child. So is it with God, we are but little children in His Hands that needs Direction for every step we should take; Therefore, When we ask God for something that we think we really need; it is my opinion that we take a step back to analyze what is it that we are really asking for and make sure that it is not because of RED EYE or ENVY, that spikes the real reason for us asking God for what we think we need.

The Bible Declares that The Disciples of Jesus Christ, when they heard and saw how He Prayed, they got to realize that all along before and present; they have never experience someone Prayed the way they saw the Messiah Prayed; which compelled them to ask Him to Teach them how to Pray to enter The Future of their lives. I first started looking into Prayer because I was Praying one day and I heard The Voice of The Lord Said to me:

"When you are Praying, I want you to Ask Me to Teach you how to Pray".

I heard what The Lord Said, but I was puzzled about what He Said; because the first thing I began to ask myself is; all along when I was Praying, was I not doing it the right way? But then The Revelation Came to me, to make me understand that there are level to everything that concerns The Almighty God; and when it is that God Is Rising an Individual to A Next Level, He then Reveals to that individual A New Way by which they should do things to Resemble The New Relationship that is now in effect with God, that brings forth A New Character.

Every New Relationship that God Introduced to Abraham, it changed the way Abraham Worshipped before God. Think it not strange People of God, has we Grow in God's Grace, we will find out, that how we walked before, will now be changed into a different walk; how we talk before, will now be Transformed; How we dressed, God's Grace will Tell us that we cannot dress that way anymore. Jacob was such a person that in order for him to Receive his Blessing and for his name to change from Jacob to Israel, it meant that he had to be determined to wrestle with God's Angel, which caused Jacob to walk a little different from how he was accustom to be walking; something he gladly accepted in order to Receive of God's Divine Blessing. Genesis 32:22-32.

Therefore, I got The Revelation, that has I climb the Ladder of Spirituality, there must be a difference in the way I speak to God. We must know by now that the natural things of this life teaches us about The Spiritual things we cannot see, because that which is natural comes from that which is Spiritual, to make us know that The Spiritual gives birth to everything that is physical. Living our lives teaches us that no one that is healthy and of a sound mind will always remain a child, but as we grow, we now manifest to be someone better than that which we were, we increase in more Understanding, in more Knowledge and in more Wisdom, and we will always find a better way to do things. My discovery of Asking God to Teach me how to Pray brought forth The Revelation of what is called The Body of Prayer; which in its own respect is indeed The Prayer that Jesus Christ Gave unto His Disciple known as The Our Father Prayer.

There is one thing that is certain in any Prayer that is Prayed, and this is; there is always a Prayer of Request, because for many of us that's the whole reason and purpose for our Prayer; not knowing that the most important Prayer to offer is a Prayer of Confessing our sins and the sin of our Forefathers and that of our Children. Without this Prayer; Prayer becomes meaningless, because everything that will be said without this Prayer will result in sin still being present in our members therefore God Cannot and Will Not Hear much less to Answer our Prayers.

Isaiah 59:1&2.

"Behold, The Lord's Hand is not shortened, that it cannot save; neither His Ear heavy, that it cannot hear: But your iniquities have separated between you and your God, and your sins have hid His Face from you, that He Will Not Hear".

Have we ever considered to ourselves that when we ask God for most of what we asked Him for, that's why it is that there is a delay, or that there is no answer to that request being asked! Have we ever considered to ourselves that there must be something wrong with what I'm asking God, concerning our lives?

I got this Testimony from someone in The Church, which I will like to share with My Readers to better understand this statement that was just made. A Sister in The Church Testified one day, and said that she does not fully understand Prayer because it is that she believes in Prayer but realize that there is a depth to Prayer that she has not yet come to understand; and this is the reason why; and she explained:

"Every time I'm really in need of something for my life that is urgent, that which I think I must have, I go on my knees to pray for God to do it for me; It does not happen or it take a long time for it to be fulfilled, or it is a situation that I'm still praying for it, with the hope that it will be answered; She continued to explained that this is where the confusion comes in: If there is someone that is in need of their deliverance or breakthrough and that person comes to her or she takes it upon herself to pray for that person; She explained that She now realize that the prayer which She have prayed for that person was answered immediately".

This is her Testimony that makes her very confused. But when I thought to consider her Testimony I got to realize that this is indeed truth, because many of us can Testify to that effect. Look on this for a minute, when we go down in Prayer for a brother or a sister in need; we must then realize that this person is standing in a position where there is no way out; except they receive help from The Almighty God; Therefore, When we Pray a Prayer in Sincerity towards God for that person who is in need, The Bible Says where two or three are gathered together touching anything concerning Me, there Am I in the midst to Answer their Prayer. And this is the flip side to this Testimony, when we are Praying for ourselves, we may not be necessarily Praying for something that will be of great benefit to us, meaning, The Spiritual man; but mainly Praying because God Says to Ask for what we need, not knowing that God Still Remains our Father that Will Not Give to us something that will harm us.

Look at this for a minute, have we ever been to the Super market, and if we were not Discipline and Wise, we may find ourselves buying a whole lot of things that we never really needed or intended to buy. For those of us that are parents, let us put our foot in The Shoe of God for a minute, as if that is even possible; but let us think for a minute, when we are in this same Super Market and there is with us our own Child that is between the age of 5-10 years old; if we ever decide to give the power to those Children to take up Groceries for the house; think on these things! What do we think the Trolley or Food basket will be filled with? You guessed it! That basket would be filled with Candy; Sweets of all different nature; and also don't forget their favourite, Chocolates. In their Minds these things are the very best things there is to eat, and no one can tell them otherwise. So is it with God and us His Children; we may think that we are Big and Mature; but truth be told, we are just Children in The Hands of God, that sees this World as a Big Super Market; and want God to Give us all that we would ask of Him to Give us. Not knowing that many of the things we are asking God for is but just Sweets; Candy and Chocolates.

These things look Good to the eyes, but if we could ever indulge in it, this will bring forth a lot of Boils; Sores and will lead to us not having proper Health to live our lives. Have we ever considered to ourselves that God Is Who He Says He Is to us, which is A Loving Father that always Cares and is Looking Out for our Benefits in life; think on these things. I have gotten to realize that God Loves me so much that all I could ever need for My Survival and for My abundant life in Him; He has already put it in store for me; it has already been Purchased, Packed and Delivered; just waiting for me to walk in My Blessing; with the little experience that I have so far Being A Child of God, I have gotten to realize that I have everything that God wants me to have; A Wonderful Wife, of which The Bible Said that he that findeth a wife findeth a good thing; Lovely Child; Good Healthy; A Home to live in; a Job to sustain me and My Family; A House of God to Worship in; and most important I have The Holy Ghost Living Inside of me, which is The Hope of Glory; think about it, what want I more. I think the biggest problem that we have, being Children of The Most High God, is that we have not yet come into Full Trust for God; therefore we doubt what God's Promise for our lives truly are.

The Topic says: LORD, What should I ask You for when I Pray? Seeing that we have illustrated so many proves that God Is Our Eternal Father that Cares for us; should we then say that there is no need to Pray! The Answer is No; that's not what I'm saying. What I'm actually saying by The Spirit of God is that we need to Mature in The Spirit, that we can Be Born in the Understanding of what we need to ask God for; which should represent that which will Edify The Spirit of God in us, rather than to Slow down or to Destroy that which God Has Given to us.

Here is a perfect example of someone Praying to God, yet being a child, but received an understanding of a wise leader to ask for a request like this. I'm talking about Solomon; He confess to The Lord that he was but a little child, knowing not how to go out or to come in; this he said after God Came to him by night, Asking him to tell Him what he wanted God to Do for him. King Solomon ask God for a Wise and Understanding heart that he may be able to judge and to lead His People. The Bible Said that God Was Moved by the request that Solomon asked, because there are so many other things that was in view for him to ask for; so is it with us has parents, if we are in the Super Market and our child choose to pick up Vegetables and Fruit instead of Sweets and Chocolates; we would then know that there is in the life of that child a Spirit from God that has Matured.

What I'm actually saying is that when we Pray, let us choose to ask wisely what is it that we are asking God for; because He Being our Good Father Will Disappoint us when we ask for something that is Foolish and Unwise. Let us save ourselves the trouble of asking and then wondering why there is a delay or why there is no answer. Let us look on the Prayer that The Lord Gave us to Pray, and try to analyze how and what He Ask us to do. St. Matthew Chapter 6:9-13. There is a part in the Prayer that says; Thy Kingdom come. Thy Will Be Done in Earth, as it is in Heaven. There it is, The Words that Says: "Thy Will Be Done"; and that, My Fellow Brethren is what we are forgetting when we are Offering our Prayers before God.

God Is Searching for this Attitude in our Prayers to make sure that in everything that we are Asking Him to Do for us; it does correspond with The Laws of God that Says Thy Will Be Done. Then and only then my brother and Sister, will Prayers Be Answered Speedily, because God's Will Is Being Done in everything we do and say. Learn this about our God, it is never what we want or need to happen; it is always what God Want and Need to take place in our lives, we are Puppets In The Hands of The Master to Fulfill His Purpose.

Isaiah 40:13. Says:

"Who hath Directed The Spirit of The Lord, or being His counsellor hath Taught Him".

When we Pray, God Recognizes exactly who we are and who's we are; because if we have grown in the Understanding and have Matured in The Spirit of God, then our conversation and Prayers Must Reflect What God's Will Is. If it does not Reflect What God's Will Is, then we are not yet Mature and are still babes in Christ. Here is a beautiful example to let us Understand even more what I'm trying to express: In The Book of Genesis Chapter 1:26. God Speaking to Himself in Thought or Said to His Heart:

"Let us make man in our Image, after our Likeness".

This God Did; and in Genesis Chapter 2:19. God Brought all the animals that were Created by Him, before Adam; the man which at that time when he was Created, knew not what it means to sin, and at the same time had The Mind of God in him; now because Adam had The Mind of God in him; every name Adam gave to the animals, that was the name indeed for that particular animal; because to have The Mind of God, it means that we think the way God Would Need us to think; therefore bringing forth God's Commandment which Says:

THY WILL BE DONE.

Is God Not Answering your Prayers! And it is, that you're His Child; this may be the problem; that which you're Asking God for, is completely out of His Will. After Adam sinned, he no longer had God's Likeness; therefore, he could no longer do things, or even think to Represent the words which Says:

THY WILL BE DONE.

I have learnt A New Prayer, when Asking God for anything; this is it:

"Lord Jesus Christ, whatever is Your Will for my life, let me have it; and whatever is not in Your Will for my life, keep it away from me; give me what is sufficient for me in a day and help me to plan only in Your Will, let Your Will Be Done in my life, Amen".

Let us keep growing together in The Fear and in The Love of The Almighty God, and remember that we are here to help each other to make it into God's Kingdom.

Give me You, everything else can wait, give me You, I hope I'm not too late. From the Servant of God, your Brother, Friend, Minister and Pastor Lerone Dinnall.

LORD, Teach Me To Only Ask For Things In Your Will.

How Fasting Should Be Conducted.

Message # 7   Done in the year 2015.

Praise Jesus Christ, all Praise goes to The Excellent God. As we have expressed an earnest desire for excellence regarding God and His Word, and to ensure that we do things in the right order, according to His Precepts and His Statues Which He Has Laid Down for us to follow. It's a Pleasure for me to channel our Minds through The Revelations of God towards the Topic Fasting.

The first Question that I would like to ask is this:

"Why Fasting"?

Before I answer that Question let me say this. I have went to a lot of Fasting services, and I have observed that even though the idea of Fasting is Maintained; I also realized that in many cases or on many occasion that Fasting is not being done the way it should be done, thus there are many people who have not received the desired results after Fasting. I know that there are many people that will read this Message and say I'm being judgemental, but before you judge me, I would ask that you read The Message first.

Those who knows about Fasting will agree that Fasting is a personal thing, except at times when you're doing a group Fasting. But we have to be concern when we realize, and have seen the prove for ourselves that there is a lot of people that are going to Church and they are not doing what they should be doing in the right way. I'm not always out spoken, but because I am now, placed in a position from God to Preach out A Ministry, I find it now as my ultimate responsibility to make sure that I do A Good Job for The Lord.

I find it quite amazing that many people who goes on Fasting actually think that Fasting is a sign which suggest that we are Holy, or that we are Righteous; this however is completely the opposite of what Fasting is about. Let's now get to the Answer of the Question that was asked: Why Fasting? We Fast because this method is the only medium through which we can get Closer to God.

Why do we need to get closer to God you may ask? The answer should be obvious, being close to God allows us to have God's Approval and Favors upon our lives. What we need to understand is that God Is Already God, and His Characteristics cannot change. One of God's Characteristic is that God Is A Holy God, therefore, His Children should ensure that they present themselves Holy at all times. And this is God Requirement. However, to answer this question even more clear; the reason why we should Fast is because of our Sin. Because of Sin, God Cannot and Will Not Get Close to His People, until the Sin is Repented of and Removed. Isaiah 59:1-4. 2 Chronicles 7:11-14.

Please note: Fasting when it is done the right way, must yield results. Now if you're a person that has been Fasting for a while, but still there is no response, the answer is simple, it is not being done the right way. Therefore, This Message will be of great importance for us, to help us to know where we fall short.

Another thing to know which is of great importance; Fasting means NO FOOD, NO WATER, NO WORK AND NO WORK BEING DONE ON OUR BEHALF. Jonah 3:6-10.

If you have to eat, it therefore means that you're not on Fasting. I find it quite interesting that there are a lot of Teachers that will Teach and Preach to Congregation telling them that they can eat a little and still be on Fasting. This Message is not true, Fasting is a Sacrifice. In life I've learned this, there is always two (2) roads in front of us, the straight and narrow road or the broad and wide road; there is right lane and there is left lane, there is up and there is down; there is right and there is wrong; there is obedient and disobedient; there is Heaven and there is hell; there is good and there is bad; there is God and there is the devil, and the list goes on. We have one life to live, let us not be like king Saul who choose to disobey God, and afterwards found himself on the wrong side of God. 1 Samuel 15:1-23.

As I said before that The Lord Has Called me to start A Ministry for Him. With this in Mind, I Accept this duty as a great privilege and see it as an honour to do something for My Father. Knowing that He Didn't have to Call me, He Could Have Chosen someone else.

With that said, I now see it as My Duty to Search The Scriptures to ensure that everything that is going to be established out of this work is done the correct way, and to the best of the knowledge that God Has Given to me. Because when we think about it, it's not just to do a job for God, but to Serve Him in the best possible way. Because if the service is not done the right way, our work is going to burn. 1 Corinthians 3:11-15.

I have here a pattern of Scriptures that is linked to Fasting, and I would call these Scriptures "The **Statues of Fasting**". We've read in Deuteronomy 6. Concerning the Statues of The Lord, which means a permanent fixture. Now I've read The Bible concerning Fasting, and I'm not here to tell you that God Cannot Give A Deeper Understanding through His Scriptures. But what I've read so far, in addition to the understanding that God Has Given me, I came up with this pattern of Scriptures, which I call The Statues of Fasting.

This simple means that this is the method that I will be using to conduct Fasting service in The Church that I am responsible for. This method will also be used by members of the Church to continue Fasting Services in this manner.

What is The Statues of Fasting you may ask? It is five (5) Scriptures with five different Sub Topics that speaks directly about Fasting as A Complete Body, they are as Follows:

The Statues of Fasting

1. The Preparation for Fasting.
2. The Quality of your Fast.
3. A Reminder that Fasting is Necessary.
4. The Accepted Fast.
5. The Expectation after Fasting.

Let's take a look at them Individually.

The Preparation for Fasting

First Scripture, St Matthew Chapter 6:16-18. As the Topic for this Scripture says The Preparation for Fasting; it is very important for a believer to know, that when we are going on a Fast, we must prepare for that Fast. For example, we have many persons that are observing a Fast, that only decide that they are going on Fasting the very morning they wake up. I've seen this one very often, when a person say the reason why I'm going on Fasting is because there is no food in the house. What St Matthew is saying, don't go on a Fast because you want to please someone or to show someone that you're observing a Fast.

To be in preparation for your Fast, you have to decide days before the Fast that this day is the day I'm going to observe a Fast. Another thing to know in preparation, we must have a reason why we Fast, a request that needs to be granted. I know that Fasting is done because of sin, but we must have a request, that after we have done the Fast correctly and Prayed, we will see the results of that Fast. It is of great importance for us to know that the Main Reason for our Fast, is to get rid of the sin, thus allowing God to finally Answer our Request. God Will Not Answer our request while sin is still present, and that is why Fasting is important, for God to Answer our Prayers.

The Quality of Your Fast

Second Scripture, Psalms 139:23-24. This Scripture speaks of a request for God to Search us the individual. But what does this have to do with quality, you may ask? When we confess to God that we give Him the permission to Search us, to Try us, and See if there be any wicked ways in us; we are actually saying to God that I have surrender my life to God, and because I have surrender my life to God, I need to make sure that I don't have anything in me now, tomorrow and forever that will stop me from Serving God. I have made up my mind, but I need God's help. We are now expressing a complete Dependence on God, to make sure that our service is of Quality. After asking God to Search us, representing a Prayer of Request, the writer which is king David then ask God to Lead him in the way Everlasting; which would suggest that we now have a complete Dependence in God, that we trust Him so much that wherever He Tells us to go, we will go and will do what He Tells us to do; no Questions Asked.

A Reminder that Fasting is Necessary

Third Scripture, Leviticus Chapter 16:29-34. This Scripture shows us that Fasting is Design and Commanded by God, for His People to do as A Continual Statue. Statues according to The Word of God, what it means is a permanent fixture that cannot and will not be changed; for example Fasting is a Statue; Prayer is a Statue; Worship is a Statue; Praise is a Statue; all these are Statues that will remain in this life until the end of time. We are reminded that Fasting is done on a special day, and also on that day we are to Afflict our soul and do No Work at all. The word afflict means to cause pain, distress, grief or misery.

Note: This is very important for us to know, afflict were Fasting is concern does not mean to induce or create harm to ourselves.

It was such a command that even those who are visiting us, if they came on the day of your Fast, they too would have to Fast, and also the stranger. This day of affliction, after it was finished, the promise was, that there would be Atonement for us, which means that our sin would be covered or cancelled. On that day would be a day of Rest, meaning that our whole focus will be on the Fast. In the Old Testament, the Priest who would represent us before God, would make the request for the Atonement; now in the New Testament, Jesus Christ died for our sin and now He is our High Priest that Mediate for us before God Almighty. That is why whatever we Pray for, we Pray in The Name of Jesus Christ. Hebrews 4:14-16. In Fasting it is necessary that we remember that Prayers and Reading of The Word of God goes hand in hand with Fasting, they all work together as one.

The Accepted Fast

Fourth Scripture, Isaiah Chapter 58. There are many people that hears about Fasting, and hears of its power to cleanse, and have desired and have done a lot of Fasting, but is still to see the desired benefits of Fasting. Here is a Scripture that tells of the Accepted Fasting that God Approve. The Scripture starts off by showing how a lot of us Fast, and yet not seeing any results, starts to blame God, saying we have done what God Asked us to do, but still there is no response. God made them know that though they say that they were Fasting, God Did Not Accept It, because it was being done for all the wrong reasons. For Example, people that were observing a Fast, was still working, and even if they were not working, those who worked for them was still working, so they were still earning from that day which should be a day of Rest. The Scripture went on to express what exactly is The Accepted Fast that should bring forth results.

And after this Fast, there are Great Benefits that will follow. In a summary format, what this Scripture is Saying is:

1. How the wicked Fast; and the response is that God Will Not Accept this Fast, Verse 1-5.
2. The purpose of the Accepted Fast, verse 6.

3. The type of Spirit that will be in us after the Accepted Fast, verse 7.

4. Verse 8-14. Speaks of the rewards of an Accepted Fast.

The Expectation After Fasting

Fifth Scripture, Leviticus Chapter 11:44-45. After Fasting, it is important to know that the expectation is not to go back to that which we were, but to move from strength to strength in God. To let us understand this more clearly, this Scripture explains the Characteristic of God, which is Holiness. Now after our Fast, we must remember that it is first design to get rid of our sin once it is done correctly; now that our sin has been removed, it gives God the opportunity to get close to us so that He Can Now Be In Fellowship to now have A Relationship with us. Now for God to Be In Fellowship with us, God Has Requirements, and that Requirement is for us to Be Holy because God Is Holy.

God Warns that after He Has Washed us from that which we were, that we should not return to that state, but rather Remain Holy because He Is Holy. If we refuse to remain clean, then God Will Refuse to Remain with us in Fellowship; and now we are back to were we started from, back in sin and far from God. Isaiah 59. What God Is Saying in this Scripture for Fasting is this, after God Have Changed us from the world; don't get conform to the things of this world, but be Transformed. Romans 12:1-2.

The Format for the Scriptures to be read in Fasting Meetings for Church:

1. St. Matthew 6:16-18.
2. Psalms 139:23-34.
3. Leviticus 16:29-34.
4. Isaiah 58.
5. Leviticus 11:44,45.

Now it is important for us to know that The Business of God is very serious, not to be taken for granted. As always God Desire for us is to come up to His Requirements. If we take five (5) years to do what is God Requirements, then it will take five (5) years for us to receive what God has in store for us.

As I have said before that I have been in a lot of Fasting service, but through reading The Bible and God Opening My Understanding, I have gotten to realize that there is more to Fasting than that which I see and was doing; therefore I thank God for His Understanding through His Scriptures, which have Empowered me to be A Better Child of God concerning His Requirements. Therefore, It is with this concept that I will be using these Statues of Fasting to conduct Fasting service in The Ministry that God Has Given to me; not only me, but also those who are a part of God's Ministry will also use this type of Teaching to conduct Fasting Service at The Church of Jesus Christ Fellowship Savannah Cross Ltd.

Question to ask, why is it that when we go to a Fasting service, the Scriptures that are read and explain has nothing to do with Fasting. When we go to a Good Friday service, the Scriptures that are read has everything to do with the death of Jesus Christ; when we go to a Christmas morning service the Scriptures that are read has everything to do with the Birth of Jesus Christ; When we go to a Lord Supper service the Scriptures that are read has everything to do with Lord supper, so why is it that when we come to a Fasting service, the Scriptures that are read don't resembles Fasting; don't you see that something is wrong. Should we not be reminded what Fasting is about, so that we can know how Fasting is to be done?

Something to remember, whenever we are going on a Fast, let us look at our self in the mirror and ask our self these questions:

1. Am I observing A Fast?
2. Am I doing the Accepted Fast?
3. Is my Heart clean from all iniquity?
4. Am I going before God to Fast?

If we can answer all these Questions in a positive way, then we can proceed with our Fast; if we cannot answer these Question in a positive way, then I can tell you before we even start the Fast, that it will be a waste of our time and energy.

I hope that this Message was A Blessing to you, and I know that this Message is a Blessing to you because you are the one who have received this Message. May God Continue to Bless and Keep you.

Praise Jesus Christ, all Praise goes to The Excellent God. From the Servant of God, Pastor Lerone Dinnall.

How Fasting Should Be Conducted.

The Danger of FORGETTING About GOD!

Message # 5   Done in the year 2015.

I Exalt and Honour The Mighty Name of Jesus Christ our Soon Coming King, Greetings and Salutation to all God's Wonderful People. It is an honour and a privilege to be writing another Message Inspired by GOD.

One of The Greatest Gift to Possess in this life is The Gift of Understanding that leads towards Receiving The Gift of Knowledge, which then Births The Gift of Wisdom. Many people would not necessarily agree with me that The Gifts Are Manifested in that order; but there is one thing that we can agree on; and this is it, that these Gifts actually does Exits.

The Danger of Forgetting about GOD; many of us look on this Topic, but do we actually Understand The Consequences of this action!

What happen when we as Children of God, do Forget about GOD? The Bible Declares in The Book of Hosea Chapter 4:6.

"My People are destroyed for lack of knowledge; because thou hast rejected knowledge, I also will reject thee, that thou shalt be no Priest to me: Seeing thou hast forgotten the law of thy God, I Will also forget thy children".

This Message is very clear, that we may know what is in The Mind of God concerning all Saints, all Nation and all Generation that makes this horrible mistake of forgetting about God. Before we go further in this Message, there are some Foundational Meanings we need to Understand about the word Forget.

FORGET: This word is a verb, which means that it requires action. According to The Webster's Dictionary, the meaning of the word Says:

"To cease to remember; to omit or to neglect ones duty or responsibilities; to fail to think of or take no note of; to neglect willfully or carelessly; to disregard or to be slight; to reject which means not to accept that which is commanded of you to do".

In The Scripture above, The Bible use the word Reject; which is to clearly show that, these people made it their decision not to do what God Had Required them to Do. And if we have found ourselves in a position such as this, then we must realize that their punishments shall also be our punishment. God Said:

"I Will Also Reject thee, and Forget thy children".

I have gotten to realize that one of the main weakness of God's People is the fact that we are prone to forget. God Also Recognize this weakness and Warns His People Continually of the Consequences they will face if they Forget about God.

Deut. 4:9&23.

"Only take heed to thyself, and keep thy soul diligently, lest thou forget the things which thine eyes have seen, and lest they depart from thy heart all the days of thy life: But teach them thy sons, and thy son's sons".

"Take heed unto yourselves, lest ye forget the covenant of The Lord your God, which He Made with you, and make you a graven image, or the likeness of anything, which The Lord thy God hath Forbidden thee".

Deut. 6:10-15

"And it shall be, when The Lord thy God Shall Have Brought thee into the land which He Sware unto thy fathers, to Abraham, to Isaac, and to Jacob, to give thee great and goodly cities, which thou buildedst not, And houses full of all good things, which thou filledst not, and wells digged, which thou digest not, vineyards and olive trees, which thou plantedst not; when thou shalt have eaten and be full; Then beware lest thou forget The Lord, which brought thee forth out of the land of Egypt, from the house of bondage. Thou shalt fear The Lord thy God, and serve Him, and shalt swear by His Name. Ye shall not go after other gods, of the gods of the people which are round about you; For The Lord thy God Is A Jealous God among you, lest The Anger of The Lord thy God be kindled against thee, and destroy thee from off the face of the Earth".

Deut. 8:11-20. This Passage of Scripture also gives Clear Instructions towards God's Commandments for us to make certain that we must never find ourselves in a Position that we have forgotten about God.

Because The LORD Realize that there is a weakness in Mankind to Forget, He Offered unto His People the only Solution which would act as an Ingredient to counteract that deadly Symptom that is Imbedded in our DNA. What is that Ingredient, you may ask? He Asked us to do A Continual Duty, which is to always remember Him, by having Feast and Celebration for what He Has Done for them and also have Done for us; and also the Main Duty was and still is, for us to Train our children, and our children's, children; that there will be no opportunity for His People to even have the thought that they will FORGET about GOD. Exodus 13:8-16. Deut. 4:1-31. Deut. 6. Deut. 11:7-32. Psalms 78:5-8.

Serving God is Great, and also Receiving of God's Blessings is Wonderful; but the Question remains, what really happens if I FORGET About GOD? Deut. 30:11-20. This passage of Scripture also reminds us that if we fail to Do what God Need us to do; then it is certain we shall surely perish, and not only us, but also our seed that follows.

I love Deut. Chapter 28:1-14. Which speaks of God's Wonderful Blessings if we Obey; but have we ever spent the time to read from Verse 15-68. To observe The Consequences for not Obeying that which God Ask of us to Obey. I can say this to you, it is Horrible, the Punishment; the Torments; the Suffering and the Curse that we must bear if we at all forget to be Obedient to The Laws, Statues and Commandments of The LORD Our GOD.

In The Book of Judges Chapter 2. There came an Angel from God Which Spoke to God's People, Telling them that The Covenant which He Had Made between God and His People is Broken; why was this so, because in The Book of Judges Chapter 1. All of The Commandments Which God Commanded Israel to Perform, they took it for granted; they Rejected it; they did not remember what God Ask them to keep; they fell out of Relationship and out of Fellowship with God; just like Adam, they fell from Grace. Therefore, God Could No Longer Hold His part of the Agreement, seeing that His People has completely forgotten about Him.

There are many Christians that believe that they carry themselves throughout the day; not knowing that it is God's Grace, His Favors and His Protection that enables us to go through that one day of our life. Truth be told, the Devil is not afraid of us; the Devil is afraid of God Almighty, I learnt that from God, when I was in a stage of my life that I wasn't Praying as often as I should. The Voice of The Lord Came to me and Said:

"Why won't you Pray more often to Me, don't you know that the devil is not afraid of you! He is only afraid of Me".

Let me tell you something, I learnt a Valuable Lesson that day; because there is many of us which believe with all our Hearts; Mind and Soul, that the Devil is afraid of us.

Further in The Book of Judges, Chapter 3:5-15. Here The Children of Israel continue to do that which is Displeasing in The Eyes of God; they took their Daughters and Sons and gave them to those of the Heathen country, people that knew not God, nor worshipped their God. They also received from these country their Sons and Daughters, and married them. This an action that God Strictly Told them not to Do. The Bible Said that The Anger of The Lord Was Hot against Israel, and He Gave them over into the hands of their enemies for eight (8) years. This is the Punishment for their Disobedience. However, when they Cried and Repented of the wrongs which they had done, The Lord Raised up men and Judges to deliver them that they will again come to Serve God.

As we are investigating what happens when we forget about God, we look forward to more activities that took place in The Book of Judges Chapter 4:1-4. This speaks of The Children of Israel doing evil before The Eyes of The Lord again; this time He Sold them into captivity for twenty (20) years with great oppressions. You would have thought that they would have learnt their lesson by now; but the answer is no. In Chapter 6:1-7. Of Judges. They Displeased God again, and The Lord Put them into the hands of their enemies for seven (7) years, this time there enemies made them very poor, to a state of poverty. At all times when their backs was against the wall, and they Cried to God, He Raised up someone to deliver them from those who oppress them; that they would again be in Fellowship with God.

It is important to point out this fact, in Judges Chapter 10:6-18. The Children of Israel again did evil in The Sight of God, to worship and to bow down before strange gods, of which He Sold them into the hands of their enemies for eighteen (18) years, of which they vexed and oppressed the Israelite that they Cried again to The Lord; but this time The Lord Send A Messenger to Speak to Israel, to remind them of how good God Was to them, but yet they Treated Him Badly; The Lord Rejected their cry for deliverance and told them to go and serve the gods which they now serve.

It is clear, and with great evidence that the last thing that we want to do has Children of God is to Forget about God. It is better that we have not known about God; than to know about Him and Displease Him in that way. We need to remember that such an act is not only for us to bear the consequences; but that the greatest part of the punishment is going to fall on our children, and our children's, children.

In The Book of Judges the main reason why The Children of Israel kept on making mistakes is because no one was persistent enough to make sure that they Do what God Had Commanded them to Do, which is to make sure that they Teach, which means to Train their children, and their children's children to come.

Somewhere along the way The Discipline to ensure that we Train and Teach is not being carried out; therefore, If it is not being carried out, you can be very sure that our lives and the lives of our children to follow will end in disappointment. The Bible is written for our

Example, with knowing this knowledge, are we going to allow the same thing that happen to The Children of Israel to happen to us!

Every Man, Woman, Parent, Pastors and Teacher have this Responsibility. What are we going to do with this Duty? Are we going to allow History to repeat itself all over again; or is it that we have decided that we are going to learn from our mistakes and ensure that we keep in Fellowship and Covenant with God. Because we must know by now that God Is No Respecter of Persons. Act 10:34 & 35. Romans 2:11.

"Then Peter open his mouth, and said, Of a truth I perceive that God Is No Respector of persons: But in every nation he that feareth Him, and worketh righteousness, is Accepted with Him".

"For there is no respect of persons with God".

Let us not keep making the same mistakes that our forefathers have made but rather let us seek to establish a future with God which sees us always prospering under The Mighty Hands of God. Let's look on me the Individual, what is it that causes me to get to a position in life that enables me to forget about God? Before I Answer that Question, look at this and consider for a minute:

Have you ever seen The Anointing of God on someone's life in great force, then few months later you happen to meet that same person, and to your surprized, that Anointing that was upon that individual's life is no longer there. You may even try to assist this person to get back on the right track, but then you get a response that says:

"I can't be bothered, or I have no more zeal in me to Serve God".

This is a touching story but also a true story; when you now seek to find out why that person can't be bothered, or why there is no zeal; you get to realize that many of the times we as Children of God Have Traded in our Salvation for Material things and for Sentiments. Things that will only last us for a time on this earth; we have Traded Everlasting Life for VAPOUR and VANITY.

Let me now answer the Question of what it is that causes us to Forget about God; the Answer is that we have TRADED. God Gave Us Eternal Life Freely, and we Traded that life for a New Car; for a House;

for a Companion; for Fame; for Money. Allow me to Declare how important Eternal Life Is; The Story of a Rich Young Ruler was told in The Book of St. Luke Chapter 18:18-30. The summary of it goes like this, the Young man came to Jesus Christ, recognizing that He Came from God; and although this young man was rich, he still realized that there was something missing in his life that his own riches could not satisfy; his good works and charity could not fill the gap, of that which was missing in his life; therefore, he came to Jesus Christ, asking him, what should he do to Inherit Eternal Life.

Just look at this fact, this Rich Young Ruler, who had all that this world could ever ask for, is asking for A Gift that God Has Freely Given to those of us that believe on His Name; look at the irony in this True Story, Those who are rich and prosperous in this world are seeking The Eternal Gift of Peace that God Has Given to us that believe on His Name; and on the other hand, those of us who have freely receive of this precious Gift, within a moment at the snap of a finger, would easily Trade this Gift that Only God Can Give.

Look at this, the Rich man never at that time Traded what he had in this life for Eternal Life, he rather to put A Value on it, even though in The Eyes of God it had no value. But still there remain many of us Christians who have not taken this story to be an example, to let us know that has the men of this World put Great value on that which they possess, so should we put an even Greater value without a PRICE TAG on The Salvation that God Has Freely Given to us.

There is a saying in this life that goes like this:

"Everything Is For Sale".

Let this not be true about our Salvation, let there not be a Price Tag on our Salvation; that suggest that it is for sale at the right price. Let's follow the Example of Daniel who knew that the decree was signed and still made Prayer before His God; Let's be like the Three Hebrew Boys that did not care what the king commandment was; but was rather determined in their Heart's, Mind and Soul that they were never going to bow to an Image that they knew was not God, even though they were warned that they would be cast into the burning fiery furnace, they did not care; I believe the Three Hebrew Boys was saying to the king:

"I'M SOLD OUT FOR GOD".

Let us as People of God be very careful that we take heed to this Message, let us not put a PRICE TAG on Our Salvation, let us not FORGET ABOUT GOD; Let the only sign that is on us Say:

"NOT FOR SALE".

The Lord Says: "If you confess Me before man, then I Will Confess you before My Father which is in Heaven; but if you deny Me, I Will Deny you".

It's simple, Stand Up for God and God Will Stand Up for you.

I Exalt and Honour The Mighty Name of Jesus Christ. May The Blessing of God Continue to be upon your life, and I hope that this Message was A Blessing to you; from The Ministry of The Church of Jesus Christ Fellowship Savannah Cross Ltd. Pastor Lerone Dinnall.

Please remember, **Do Not Forget About God**.

The Danger of FORGETTING About GOD.

We Will Never Become Better Christians Until We've Overcomed The Power and The Sentiments of Money.

Message # 34   Written in the year 2015.

Greetings in The Matchless Name of Jesus Christ Our Soon Coming King; it is always an honour to be writing to you concerning Messages that The Lord Has Inspired.

It's safe to say that we are living in a world that is money orientated; as it is right now, there is nothing we can do in this world that does not attract the use of MONEY. And because there is such a great emphasis on money, it can be said that money has taken the focus of our MINDS; therefore, no longer do we have earnest desire to Please God when we wake up in the morning, but now that desire is change from God, to what is the quickest action that we can take, to ensure that enough money is made to maintain our lifestyle.

We must remember that The Bible Said that the lovers of money is the route to all evil. What am I saying? Is it that money is not good and we should not desire to have it! No; that's not what I'm saying. But rather I'm Expressing that we should seek to love God above all things and never let the influence of money or anything else, take over that love that we have for God. One of the main thing we allow money to do is to take over God's First Place in our lives, in such a way that we even rise from sleep in the morning and forget to have Devotion with our God.

I can speak of this Testimony because I was a person that allowed money and success to consume My life that I almost forgot about early Morning Devotion which brings forth True Relationship with God. It was not until The Lord Took Away Success; Money; and Opportunity that I realized that the only thing that remains was still My Devotion with God, that which I was neglecting so much. God Taught me a valuable lesson to know that My Relationship with Him is The Most Valuable Possession that I could ever have.

I remembered before I receive a job, I was a person that was in Prayer Meeting every morning Prayer Meeting was being held, which is on Tuesdays and on Thursdays. I remember I was still going to Prayer Meeting when I got the job but after a while I forgot about Prayer Meeting, I remember that there was service every night of the week, but when I got the job, My Service for God became smaller and smaller; therefore God Had to Make Me Know, What and Who was really Important. But I am happy for My Experience because I now have a set of Young People in The Church that The Lord Is Allowing Me to Train them to become better men and women for the future; and if they are willing to be Trained to Be Better, I know that their future will be bright and filled with The Joy of The Lord.

Many people don't understand that the aim for training the youths is to make sure that they do not make the same mistakes that we have made; this is the Main Purpose for The Bible, which Teaches us about the Past Experience of our Forefathers, thus we will not grow to make the same mistakes in the Future.

The Lord Used a term in The Topic that Says: "We'll never be better Christians". This part of The Topic caught My Attention. But when I seek to understand why The Lord Used the term Better; My Investigation allowed me to understand a little of what is in The Mind of God. And this is what The Lord Revealed to me:

1. Everyone has an understanding of what A Christian is and should be, many persons will give of their own understanding by Revealing what they think is the way of an ideal Christian. If we should speak to other Individuals concerning this Topic, they will tell us something else according to their revelation and their understanding from God. And because it was Revealed to them in that way, they would never take the time out to consider what is in The Mind of God to Establish Deeper Revelations;

    NOTE: One Revelation does not bring forth an end to our growth or to receive more Revelations from God; with God there is always more Revelations.

2. It is God that Truly Knows who it is, that are His Children.

3. Not because brother (A) is able to Preach a better Sermon than brother (B); this does not esteem brother (A) a more worthy Christian than brother (B) in God's Eye. Here is a Secret that The Lord Revealed to me; whenever a Preacher goes forth to give God's Message, The Message is for that Preacher first before it reaches the congregation; the Preacher is always the first person that needs fixing, because The Word of God is for everyone, none is excluded.

4. Everything in life must be looked on in a way in which God Would View the situation and not man. The Example was given to us by The Lord in The Bible when Samuel wanted to Anoint the eldest son of Jesse to be King, saying to those in attendance, "Surely The Lord's anointing is before him"; this we learnt that this was not God's View, but rather the sight of man. 1 Samuel Chapter 16:1-13.

    They never even consider the young man David, because in their eyes God Can Never Choose him, because they did not choose him.

Can we see the problem that most of us have in our members, we became JUDGE: JURY AND EXECUTIONER; and leave God behind, when all God Ask us to Be is Christ Like. There is a passage in The Bible, after the Resurrection, John ask Jesus Christ:

"Which is he that betrayeth thee, what shall this man do". St John Chapter 21:20-22.

Jesus Response to him Was: "If I will that he tarry till I come, what is that to thee".

In other words God Was Saying to him that, what doesn't concern you leave it alone, your job is not to count the fault and to look on those who have made mistakes; but your job is to be an example. And that's a Revelation that many of us have not yet observed.

5. Within The Eyes of God All Believers are walking on a Scale to Become CHRIST LIKE; but to what measurement we are on that scale only God Alone Can Tell.

6. Therefore, when God Said that we need to be Better Christians, He Is Clearly Saying that all of us is on a scale that measures our quality of being Christ Like; and God Is Saying unto us that we can do better because there is always room for improvements. There is a Scripture in St Matthew Chapter 5:20. Which Says:

"Except your righteousness shall exceed righteousness of the Scribe and Pharisees, ye shall in no case enter into the Kingdom of Heaven".

This is not the time to be watching others, and if someone is in The Church, that do not seek to lift their level of Worship; that does not mean that we should not lift our level of Worship or Attitude towards God in a Positive way. Remember at all times that God Needs us to Become BETTER, and not to remain at the same place being Stuck in Our Spiritual Growth.

There is a Parable that Jesus Christ Spoke, in regards to The Master which gave to His servants talents to work on; He gave one person five talents; He gave to another two talents; and to another He gave one talent. The person with the one talent decided to remain the same, while the remaining two persons worked on their talents, and earned 100% benefit for their efforts. St. Matthew Chapter 25:14-30. The Lord Also Said in the 48th Verse of St. Matthew Chapter 5; that we must therefore be Perfect, even as your Father which is in Heaven Is Perfect.

7.   These words Declare The Expectation of Our Heavenly Father, which is Perfection and only perfection is accepted from all His Children.

The first thing we need to look on concerning the power of money, is the fact that we are the individuals that gives money this power over our lives. It is important for us to Understand that every answer that we would ever need is already in The Bible, but we are not seeking The Knowledge of God to Understand His Messages, which is The Engrafted Words that is able to save our Souls. The power of money comes from us; let us have a look at these words:

"THOU SHALT NOT COVET THY NIEGHBOUR HOUSE; LAND; WIFE; CHILDREN AND WHATEVER BELONGS TO THY NEIGHBOUR".

Many of us can call this commandment a state of being RED EYE.

Many of us that are working cannot say that we have not Earned, and also, that we don't have the access to receive money. We then get to realize that the problem is in us, because we LUST so much after other people progress and success in life, that we are fuel with lust which tells us that at any cost possible, I must achieve what another person have achieve in their lives; and because we are burning with lust we will do whatever it takes to ensure that we have every chance available to receive that which we are burning with desire for, therefore giving unstoppable power to that which we call the spirit and hunger to receive more money to satisfy our greed. It is the Influence of money which creates and breaks opportunity; it brings forth advantages, and also makes mountain of disadvantages that causes all those who are caught under its web to find it very difficult to climb the ladder of what we assume to be success. And this is what we have not realized, all that desire to have; allows us to put a lot of focus on that which is Vanity, and place our God that only Accepts First Place, in second or third or fourth place; you get the idea; a position He Will Not Accept. God Is Only First or nothing at all!

This Message is not to say that God Does Not Need for us to be successful in life, no that's not what The Lord Is Establishing. The Bible Declares that I Came that ye may have life and have it more abundantly. I'm speaking about the lusting that causes hunger to desire more at any cost.

The Bible Say: "What shall a man give in exchange for his soul, shall he gain this whole world only to lose his own soul".

Think about it, when we run after money; can Money, Opportunity, Success, House, Car and Business; can all these things on the final day allow us to be Saved. The Answer is clear. _____.

There is a wise man in The Book of Proverbs 30; he goes by the name Agur; he Cemented wise words coming from The Mouth of God, that teaches us how we should live being A Child of God. It is full time we try to understand the importance of this Message from Agur for our lives. In Verse 8. This is what he Said:

"Remove far from me vanity and lies: Give me neither poverty nor riches; feed me with food convenient for me".

This request from Agur completely kills the power and influence of money and self-desire in his life. This The Lord Spoke by the mouth of this wise man, to let us know that any other request that goes beyond this, will result in God's Children going outside of The Will of God to receive our LUST.

Here is a List of Inspiring Thoughts from The Word of God:

"Better is little with the Fear of The Lord, than great treasure and trouble therewith". Proverb 15:16.

"Better is a little with righteousness than great revenues without right". Proverb 16:8.

"Better is the poor that walketh in his uprightness, than he that is perverse in his ways, though he be rich". Proverb 28:6.

All these Scriptures are speaking to us regarding the power of money that drives us out of The Will of God; but look at this Scripture: Proverb 10:22.

"The Blessing of The Lord, it Maketh Rich, and He Addeth no Sorrow with it".

The Bible Encourage us that we should seek ye first The Kingdom of God and all His Righteousness and then all things will be added unto us. St Matthew Chapter 6:25-34.

Truth be told, many of us are caught in a web that allows us to be blinded towards the Spiritual things of God, which allows us to be Programed to seek all this world riches before we seek God, not knowing that the moment we make the CHOICE to accept riches of this world over God, that's the very moment we become poor and have lost God forever; but thanks be to God for a word that is called MERCY, which gives to all man a SECOND CHANCE.

I can say this because I was such a person that never understood that which God Needed for me to do for Him, that it must be done First; therefore I am a Living Testimony that got my second chance; and I can say to all believers that are seeking to follow God, to let them know that doing what God Need for us to Do for Him comes FIRST, or else God Will STOP every progress in our lives until we have accomplished that which He Asked of us to Accomplish.

Can I tell the Saints What God Did to me! He Withheld everything in His Hands that I desired to have, and Told me that I Will Receive it as soon as I have completed what He Has Instructed me to Do for Him. Therefore, I testify to all Saints that are reading this Message; Don't Try To Go Around God; just do exactly what He Tells you to Do. The Word of The Lord Says in Psalms 127. Except The Lord Build the House, they labour in vain that build it.

Please remember that passage of Scripture the next time you're seeking to do something without The Permission of God; it will all be in VAIN, if God Has Not Stamp His Approval on whatever you're doing; IT'S A VAIN SHOW.

How does it feels to know that you have done something but it was not being done at its very best? I know how I would feel; Unsatisfied, The Message Says:

"We will never become better Christians until we have overcome the power or sentiments of Money".

I can't speak for My Readers, but I desire to be THE BEST CHRISTIAN that I can possibly Become. The Bible Said that we know not what we shall be, but this we know that we shall be like Him.

To Be Christ Like, are we ready for The Change? Or is it just a word that flows off our lips! One thing I can declare, when we have Become the Christians that God Need us to Become, then and only then will we be considered to be ROYAL; HOLY; and SPECIAL in The Eyes of God; then and only then will the Words be upon us that says, before ye call, I Will Answer; and while your speaking I Will Hear. Then and only then will these words be for us:

"Greater Is He that is in you than he that is in the world; greater works than these which I have done shall ye do because I go to My Father".

I thank you for taking the time out to read this Message, I hope that this Message opened the eyes to your Soul, and all of us together will desire to reach the mark of PERFECTION one step at a time. God's Blessings always. From the Servant God, I remain your Brother; Your Friend; Your Minister; Your Pastor Lerone Dinnall.

Becoming Better Christians.

A Time For Tithing.

Message # 40   **Date Started December 14, 2016**
                                Date Finalized December 29, 2016.

All Honour, Glory and Power Forever and ever to The Only Living GOD; I greet My Lord and Saviour Jesus Christ, I greet all My Brothers and Sisters in The Lord; glad am I, glad am I, no stranger to The Fellowship of Our Lord and Saviour Jesus Christ; with great Respect I count this privilege as a wonderful opportunity, to be able to be in the position to write another Inspiring Message for God's People, and also for my children that is now, and for those future Generation to come.

There is one main thing that must be understood by those of us who are Christians, and that is; if God Is Pleased with our Service being His Instruments, then God Will No Doubt Ensure that there will be A Continuation to come from our Loins, so that the Taste of True Service can be Maintained for future Generations. Now the Maintaining of The Sacrifice strongly depends on us who are now living for God, because the Generation to come will not know what it is to offer an Excellent Sacrifice to God, unless we that are living now have already learnt how to Offer The Excellent Sacrifice for God, that we will be in a Position to Train the upcoming Generation in the right path to walk.

Here we have A Topic, Which Says: "A Time For Tithing". I felt compelled, being now a Pastor of my own Assemble to write about this Topic; there is a lot of Questions that comes my way, not only on the Topic of Tithes, but a lot of other Questions, that demands that I should have suitable Answers, to satisfy the Members of The Church Family, thus resulting in me being in this position that I find myself writing a lot of Messages, to satisfy the Questions that members are asking and is seeking to find the right Answers to Solidify their Christian walk.

Tithing, while it is very necessary, it is not A Topic I personally seek to Preach on a lot; reason being, I am called to be an Officer for God, and the last thing that I need to be the center of My Attraction is the Influence of Money and Gifts in The Church. Because we've got to be very careful when it concerns the Business of The King of kings and Lord of all lords. I remember receiving A Warning from God, when I first got the Commission to go forth and to Build an Altar for God; The Lord Reminded me of the story of the Disobedient Prophet, to be found in The Book of 1 King Chapter 13. The Lord Reminded me that I must be an Example for Him and only God, not myself, or else! The Bible Warns that a Servant of God must be an Example, in 1 Timothy 3:1-13. Verse 2&3, explains:

"A Bishop then must be blameless, the Husband of one Wife, vigilant, sober, of good behavior, given to hospitality, apt to teach; not given to wine, no striker, **NOT GREEDY OF FILTHY LUCRE**; but patient, not a brawler, not covetous".

Now considering that The Bible Said that the love for Money is the root to all evil, and gifts blinded the eyes of the Righteous; I rather to put most of My Attention on The Words of God, to be always in a Position that I can search The Words, to identify what I should be doing, from what I should not be doing, in order to ensure that The Altar that The Lord Asked me to Build is in no way Compromised by the Influence of Money or Gifts.

Building an Altar, the truth is, we desire an Altar that True Worshippers can be found, and it doesn't matter if The True Worshipper rage in the amount of being only twenty (20) persons, in a building that should accommodate two Hundred (200) persons; we have got to start to identify that God Is Seeking for THE TRUE WORSHIPPERS, those that will come forth to offer The Sacrifice in Spirit and in Truth. If God Is Indeed Seeking for True Worshippers; why are we satisfied with anything and everything; then The House of The Living God will then become a den of thieves, and Money Exchangers, and Merchant Sellers. The Bible Said that if I Be Lifted Up, then I Will Draw all men unto Me; it is God that Does the Drawing; it is God that Sends The Glory. If there is an Assembly with twenty (20) True Worshippers, we would be amazed at The Glory and the Blessing that their Tithes and Offering brings to The House and Ministry of God.

Obtaining or Attracting True Worshippers is the KEY when speaking about A Topic of this Delicacy; the truth is, Tithes or the Giving of Tithes; make an observation on the word GIVING, which means that it's an Offering, and it must be done by a FREE and WILLING Mind and Heart; or else whatever we have given will not be Accepted, even though there is the evidence there to prove visually that we have participated in the giving of our Tithes and Offerings. We have got to remember that it is God that Does the Measuring, not a book that does the recording of what is collected, therefore God Knoweth the Hearts and Minds of His People that comes forth with An Accepted Free Will Offering.

Let us seek to remember the story of the Widow's mite? St Luke 21:1-4. Everyone came and gave of their abundance, but this poor Widow came and gave of all that she possessed; and The Lord Identified, and Made Notice to His Disciples of what took place in the life of the Widow; so is it when we come forth to Give Our Sacrifice to God; God Knows, even when no one else knows. One of the first things we should be thinking of where Tithes is concern, is a word that is called Appreciation for God and for His Work; Tithing is built with the Ingredience of Relationship with God.

The same way we Treat God, it will be identified in the way that we Give to God a FREE WILL Offering, which will result in the same way that God Will Treat us, in referring to God's Divine Blessings. Psalms 18:25&26.

"With the merciful Thou Wilt Shew Thyself Merciful; with an upright man Thou Wilt Shew Thyself Upright; with the pure Thou Wilt Shew Thyself Pure; and with the froward Thou Wilt Shew Thyself Froward".

Let us ask ourselves this Question: If I Treat God Without Respect, will God Then Respect me? _____.

I was Ministering to someone the other day, and I was speaking on The Topic of Offering; I remember saying to that person that no one in this World can hold down a person that Offers to God A Free Will Offering. The Offering of our Service, the Offering of our time for God, the Offering of our Bodies as A Living Sacrifice, our Offering of Money and Gifts to The Work of The Lord. Though a lot of people will try their very best to keep down a person like this; it will never work, and can never work in the Future to come; because when there is in us the Mind and the Heart to Give to God an Excellent Sacrifice; God Then Imparts on our lives, God's Divine Blessing, which is God's Greatest Favors. Which leaves others to wander what is it that we are doing that they are not doing to receive of the same Favors that we are enjoying; some will even seek to pattern everything that we have done and is doing, In the event that they now can receive of the Abundant Blessings that God Has Bestowed upon our lives. And then when the patterning does not work, because it wasn't coming from a Free Will Heart and Mind; then it will be realized that, what The Servants of God are doing for God is indeed coming from the Mind and the Heart in a Free Will manner.

I have A Testimony that I will share with you: I was told by my Mother and Her close Friends that when I was conceived in the womb, My Mother did everything in her power to terminate the pregnancy, and after trying three times unsuccessful, she was warned to leave the child alone because God Has A Purpose for this child. Before I got Saved, The Lord Gave My Mother A Vision of me with Angels Surrounding me in the sky; then she understood that God Indeed Had A Purpose for my life, and she knew I was going to Get Saved. I share this Testimony with you to make you know that if you're a person that is Destined to Offer to God Excellent Sacrifice; not even your mother while you're in the womb, can do anything to stop that Offering from being fulfilled. Nothing and No one can do anything to prevent our purpose from being fulfilled, because our Purpose is Sealed by GOD. This however will not stop the enemy from fighting, which may seem to our eyes that our Blessing is being prevented; but the Truth is, it is only being delayed until we have reached an accepted Anointing to be able to manage that particular Blessing. But every Blessing for God's People has its Perfect Harvest. The Big Question is, are we Discipline enough to do what is necessary and to wait on God's Time.

A Time for Tithing, what does this means? The Bible Declare in The Book of Ecclesiastes Chapter 3:1.

"To everything there is a season, and a time to every purpose under the Heaven". Verse 6 says: "A time to get, and a time to lose; a time to keep, and a time to cast away".

Before I came to the conclusion that I must do A Message on Tithing, I Consulted The Lord by Asking what should The Topic be called, and what would The Message be focused on; and The Lord Said, it shall be called A Time For Tithing, and the Focused shall be that of HOLINESS. This Topic should make reference for us to understand that in all that God Has Given to His People, there is still The Requirement from God, that He Requires something in return coming from A Willing Mind and Heart of His People, to show forth the debts of the Relationship between God and His People. The Lord Also Revealed that if there is not the Evidence to support that our life is now Blessed from The Ministry that seeks to Present us to God, then there is no need for us to give a Contribution of any sort to represent Tithing; because Tithing can only be offered if indeed that we have Proven that God Is Now A Blessing for our lives. Genesis 28:10-22, make reference to this Revelation. Verse 20-22 of the same Chapter explains.

"And Jacob vowed a vow, saying, If God Will Be With me, and Will Keep me in this way that I go, and Will Give me bread to eat, and raiment to put on, so that I come again to my father's house in peace; then shall The Lord be my God: and this stone, which I have set for a pillar, shall be God's House: and of all that Thou shalt give me I will surely give the Tenth unto thee".

It is also made mention of in The Book of Genesis Chapter 14:18-20.

"And Melchizedek king of Salem brought forth bread and wine: and he was The Priest of The Most High God. And he Blessed him, and said, Blessed be Abram of The Most High God, Possessor of Heaven and Earth: and Blessed be The Most High God, which hath Delivered thine enemies into thy hand. And he gave him Tithes of all".

Seeing that it may take a while for a Christian to truly identify that their life is now a Blessing, because becoming a Blessing depends on the fact that we are Discipline Enough to follow after Holiness; this action will explain the Title of The Topic which says, A Time for Tithing. I know we have been taught that everything we earn and do must be made accountable for giving back to God His Tenth; but God Has Revealed that a person who is structured to give without knowing the meaning of why they are giving, and not knowing the Revelation of the Relationship in Tithing, it will be of no benefit to that person; any Wind and Storm that comes the way of that person will allow that person to have a change of Mind and Heart towards making that Sacrifice of Tithing.

A Christian who is now Born in the Revelation of knowing the Importance of Tithing to their Relationship with God and their future Generation, and I said with God, not The Pastor or Ministers or Missionaries or Saints; this person will have the Greatest of Benefits from God, because their Relationship with God will be one that no one can break or even stop them from Offering what is Deserving of God to Receive.

Tithes is considered to be The First and The Best, also Tithes in The Eyes of God, given by someone who is considered Worthy, will represent A Holy Sacrifice before God. It therefore means that many of us, though it is that we have made the physical evidence to confirm that we have given; if we are ignorant of what Holiness is, and the Appreciation of accepting the knowledge to give to God what is Best and First, then we have only wasted our precious time in completing a Ritual / Custom that will be of no benefit to us; it would be better if we had taken the money or the time of our sacrifice, and use it for our own benefit because it would not have benefited us in The Eyes of God. God Moves in A Direction Towards that which Is Holy, God Sees What Is Holy, God Can Feel What Is Holy, God Smells What Is Holy, God Taste What Is Holy, which leads to God Accepting What Is

Holy by The Manifestation of The God Head, Being Understanding, Knowledge and Wisdom.

Tithing is not a Competition, because we identify someone giving their Tithes, it brings forth jealousy for us wanting to do the same thing that another person is doing. Tithing is a Serious Offering that must be entered into being the likeness of A Vow before God that will be given from a Holy and Free Willed Mind and Heart. There must not be any Pressure presented for a person to Offer to God their Tithes, because The Tithes Is Holy, that means it does not belong to us, it is for God and for the Continuation of His Work on Earth.

It is of great importance that while looking to discover and to understand the meaning and the purpose of Tithing, and also to understand the Topic given which says A Time for Tithing; it is of extreme importance that The Topic of Offering be looked at, to better understand the importance of Tithing.

Let us take a look on this Example: Let's put ourselves for a minute, viewing what God is Seeing each day: A child that is being taken care of by his or her mother, of which the Parents of that child tries their very best to ensure that this child is well cared for; breast feeding in its proper measurement, clothing and shelter and especially love, and the most Important Ingredience, which is to Train the child in The Will of God. In another viewing, The Lord Identify that there is a Parent or Parents of a child that seeks not to do what is meaningful and recommended for the growth of their child, and while it is that the nourishments are not given, the worst part is that there is not the Influence to ensure that the child is grown in The Fear of God. Now if these two children is representing two plants before God; which one of the Plant will have a Bright and Productive future in The Eyes of God? _____.

I shared this equation for us to understand that when we are coming to God with an Offering; if The Lord Identify that the fruits of the Offering is not Worthy, then it will not be Accepted. The story of Cain and Abel best describe this knowledge. Genesis 4:1-15. Verse 3-7 explains:

"And in process of time it came to pass, that Cain brought of the fruit of the ground an Offering unto The Lord. And Abel, he also brought of the Firstlings of his flock and of the fat thereof. And The Lord Had Respect unto Abel and to his Offering: but unto Cain and to his Offering He Had Not Respect. And Cain was very wroth, and his countenance fell. And The Lord Said unto Cain, Why art thou wroth? And why is thy countenance fallen? If thou doest well, shalt thou not be accepted? And if thou doest not well, sin lieth at the door. And unto thee shall be his desire, and thou shalt rule over him".

I find in the World at present, that many people are of the Cain spirit and attitude; they want the Best that God Has to Offer but they are just not willing to give to God of their Best. And the opportunity is there for all to accept the chance to Give to God of their very Best. But if it is that we are Offering to God A Free Will, Holy Sacrifice, then there is nothing that can stop God from Accepting our Sacrifice, which then will bring forth our Divine Blessing.

Christians that understand how to Offer The Accepted Holy Sacrifice are BOLD Christians, because we know deep down that even though the enemy say he's going to destroy us, we know by The Word of God that it cannot work because we are Standing on The Foundation, The Rock which is The WORD of GOD. Heaven and Earth shall pass away, but My Words shall never pass away, it Stands Forever. The Lord Said that He Honors His Words above all His Names. What are those words saying about The Promises that God Has Made for all those who are TRUE WORSHIPPERS.

Romans 8:31 Says:

"What shall we then say to these things? If God be for us, who can be against us?"

Every Offering that is given, if it is Holy, it goes towards the Building and Manifestation of God's Glory; every Offering that is given and is not Holy, it is then Rejected and has no purpose in The Manifestation of The Building of God's Glory. You will find at times that The Church Receives Contribution, but soon after realize that whatever The Church tries to do with that Contribution it is just not Productive. If we think about it, is this God's Way of Telling His People what is an Accepted Offering, from that which is a Rejected Offering; think about it.

If we could ever see what God Sees, when someone comes to us in good faith to give us an Offering or a Gift; if we could see that person behind closed doors or away from our presence; what is said and what is Complained, what is Murmured and what is done in secret pertaining to spiritual wickedness and powers concerning what they had given under the guise to be a snare for God's People, which spells one word, and that one word is INIQUITY; then if we could see, we would not have Accepted what was given to us by so called good faith, because that Gift or Offering will in no form be of any Benefit to the person that received it. But if that which is given to us came from someone that is A True Worshipper, then there is no worries because the Title of A True Worshipper is not one that is given or spoken over someone life, but it is a Title that is Earned by reaching A Qualified State in The Eyes of GOD.

True Worshippers cannot give and then go behind your back and Murmur, A True Worshipper has no Appetite to Complain or Watch and Count that which they have Given to God or to someone in need, because their Manifestation comes from God being only PURE. Therefore, Receiving Offerings and Gifts from A True Worshipper, will only bring forth Productive Fruits which must be A Blessing to our lives and The Ministry of God. By their Fruits ye shall know them; therefore you can actually gage the progress of when we receive Gifts or Offerings from someone; if it is that Blessing Springs from that Gift or Offering that we have Accepted, then we can mark that person as A True Worshipper; but if after we have received that Gift or Offering, there is absolutely no Blessing, but instead Destruction and a Curse, and also Snares; then we should also mark that person to make sure that we no longer receive from their hands any Gifts and Offerings presented to us and our Family and The Church Ministry.

We are The Sons of God, if God Refuse Gifts and Offerings, as He did by Telling the Prophet Malachi to tell His People to Offer their Sacrifice to their Governor instead of God, to see if the Governor will accept what they were giving to The Almighty God; Malachi Chapter

1. We being His Offspring's by His Spirit should be able to Discern what is Good from that which is Evil, and do likewise to Refuse that which is not Acceptable. What am I saying? Is it that I'm trying to let God's People realize and acknowledge that there is actually Gifts and Offering given with evil and secret intentions! That instead of Building The Work and Kingdom of God on Earth, those Gifts and Offering instead delay or prevent The Glory of God to come forth; we better believe that it is True.

But this Command will not be received by many, because many people are still Ignorant of the Devices of the devil, or maybe it is that we have not yet reached the Level for God to Reveal that Secret to us. Did not God Say to king David that although he had good intentions of wanting to Build The House of God, The Lord Response to king David is that he couldn't Build The House of God, but He Will Allow his son to Build The House of God instead. By trying to understand why The Lord Said that; it must be because king David was a man of war and had shed a lot of Blood.

Take a look at this example: If someone brought forth a Christmas Gift at our home, and we open that Gift and found a poisonous Snake inside, that springs out to destroy our Family; will we be happy, would we be smiling, will we now be desirous to receive any other Gifts from the hands of that person? On the other hand, if a True Worshipper brought us a Gift for Christmas, and before we open that Gift we can feel the Confirmation of The Holy Ghost that this is an Accepted Gift, then when we would have open that Gift it springs forth Blessings and Favors, as if it is coming from God Himself.

Which of these two Gifts or Offering would we consider to be A Blessing and would desire to Accept a second or third time at the hands of that person who gave it? This is The Privilege of God to Know who is Worthy from who is not Worthy; who is Holy from that person who is not Holy; who is A True Worshipper from those who are Pretending to be True Worshippers. And believe me, there is a lot of Pretenders; they Preach, they Pray, they Teach, they go to Church, they Give their Tithes and Offering, they keep The Lord's Supper, they attend the Fasting Services, they wrap themselves up to be Angels of Light, they are even our so called best friends, when in fact they are really Darkness covering themselves up to be Light.

2 Corinthians 11:13-15.

"For such are false Apostles, deceitful workers, transforming themselves into the Apostles of Christ. And no marvel; for Satan himself is transformed into an angel of light. Therefore it is no great thing if his ministers also be transformed as the ministers of Righteousness; whose end shall be according to their works".

God Knows, that is why only God Can Be God; and those who are Serving God without Pretending, God Will Reveal the Secrets to The True Worshippers, that they may know what to keep away from, that has been fully disguised from the eyes of the physical man. Therefore, when The Lord Ask us to Stay Away from certain things or Individuals, we must TRUST GOD'S JUDGEMENT, because God Alone Knows what take place in the Crystal Ball of the Future and in the Dark Places that no physical eye can see.

I need My Readers to understand that one of the perfect way to hide or reveal a person's true Character is through the Offering and Gifts that comes from their hands. God Alone Knows the Manifestation of the Mind and Hearts of Individuals, therefore He Knows what to Accept and what to Reject. God knows what to Allow The True Worshippers to be involved with or in, and what the True Worshippers should be kept from.

Did not Jesus Christ Accepted a man that was in the process of burying his father, Saying: Come and follow Me, let the dead bury their dead. And before that took place in the same story a man willingly came to Jesus Christ saying wherever thou go I will follow thee; the response to this man was Rejection by saying, Foxes have hole, birds have nest, but The Son of man have not where to lay His Head. Who knows what the Intention of the first man was, but God Knew, and God Decided that He had no need for his Service / Offerings; on the other hand, The Lord Compel the young man to follow Him even though he was about to Bury his father and asked permission to bury his father first, God Was Not Going to wait because He Had Need of this young man's Service, because his Service / Offerings would be one that GOD ACCEPTS. Again there was a third man that came to Jesus Christ, saying that he will follow Him, but he needed permission to go home to bid his friends and family farewell, he also was met with Rejection; The Lord Told him that no man having put his hand to the plough, and looking back, is fit for The Kingdom of God. St Luke Chapter 9:57-62.

It is Reported in The Book of Numbers Chapter 13 and Chapter 14. That The Lord Told Moses His Servant to send men to spy out the Promise Land, of which Moses choose twelve (12) men according to the number of the Tribe of Israel; these men went and did as Moses Commanded them to do, and came back after (40) days, and when Moses asked them to Report what they had seen of the Promise Land; Ten (10) men of the twelve(12) that was sent Reported an evil Report that brought fear to the ears of all those who were receiving their Report. Only Caleb and Joshua stood up and acknowledge that the Reports that was given is false; take a note of this, they STAND UP for what was Right and Honest. This action however by the ten (10) men, along with the people that hanged on everything that was spoken from their mouths, resulted in God Cursing that whole Generation from twenty years upward from entering at that time in the Land that was Provided for them by God. That Generation of people all died in the Wilderness, except for Caleb and Joshua, they were the only two men that Stand Up for Righteousness, an Offering that God Willingly Accepted, which resulted in Great Benefits and also a Leadership Position for the man Joshua.

I want us to recognize that we indeed can make a Difference amongst much people that are not believers of Christ; Caleb and Joshua did so, and they were Rewarded for their efforts. The other ten men with all the other people of their Tribe, at that time when they were Complaining and Murmuring and telling lies; this was an Offering that they were Giving to God without realizing that an Offering is not only given at The Altar at the time of Sacrifice but in a person every Walk and every Talk, every Decision and every Conclusion, every Conversation and every Mindset, every Heart desire to lust. Therefore, we have to be very careful of the Offerings that comes from our lives, it may be that we have sinned and cause God to Refuse to Accept our Sacrifice.

Have a look at The Offering that was a Rejection.

Number 14:26-37.

"And The Lord Spake unto Moses and unto Aaron, saying, how long shall I bear with this evil congregation, which murmur against Me? I Have Heard the murmurings of the Children of Israel, which they murmur against Me. Say unto them, As truly as I Live, Saith The Lord, as ye have spoken in Mine Ears, so Will I Do to you: your carcases shall fall in the wilderness; and all that were numbered of you, according to your whole number, from twenty years old and upward which have murmured against Me, doubtless ye shall not come into the land, concerning which I sware to make you dwell therein, save Caleb the son of Jephunneh, and Joshua the son of Nun. But your little ones, which ye said should be a prey, them Will I Bring in, and they shall know the land which ye have despised".

Verse 36 & 37 says: "And the men, which Moses sent to search the land, who returned, and made all the congregation to murmur against him, by bringing up a slander upon the land, even those men that did bring up the evil report upon the land, died by the plague before The Lord".

Have a look on **The Accepted Offering**:

Numbers Chapter 14:6-9.

"And Joshua the son of Nun, and Caleb the son of Jephunneh, which were of them that searched the land, rent their clothes: and they spake unto all the company of the children of Israel, saying, the land, which we passed through to search it, is an exceeding good land. If The Lord Delight in us, then He Will Bring us into this land, and Give It us; a land which floweth with milk and honey. Only rebel not ye against The Lord, neither fear ye the people of the land; for they are bread for us: their defence is departed from them, and The Lord Is With us: fear them not".

Verse 38 says: "But Joshua the son of Nun, and Caleb the son of Jephunneh, which were of the men that went to search the land, lived still".

Getting back to Tithes; now that we have an understanding about Offerings and Gifts; to actual be in a position to give Tithes will be easier to accept in order to give.

Note: I found this information concerning Tithes, coming from The Illustrated Manners and Custom of The Bible: which says, and I quote:

"Every Spiritual Relationship of a man is expressed in some material way". End quote.

If we should read The Book of Deuteronomy Chapter 26:4-12. We will identify that there was this great sense of Gratitude coming from all God's People that have Recognized that their lives is now in the category of Being A Blessing by God, therefore they saw it to be a Pleasure to have the opportunity to Give back to God what God Had Ask for them to Give. A humbleness of Heart and Mind was expressed by those who would Offer their Tithes. They thanked God for His Deliverance of their Forefathers; they thanked God for Delivering in times of need; they thanked God for Delivering them from the hands of those who Oppressed them; and also thanked God for the Blessing of which they have received and is enjoying.

Note: The Tithes of A True Worshipper must go towards The Place or The Ministry that we have identified that our Blessing flows from; towards A Servant of God or Ministry that we have identified has being A Priest for The Ministry of God's Glory.

Note: If The Priest of God is not Standing in the path to Please God, by Representing The True and Living God, then that Priest or Ministry cannot Stand and will not Stand in the Place to Accept the Tithes coming from the True Worshippers, because the True Worshipper will not Receive A Blessing for their Offering and Tithes if God Does not Grant The Approval of the Priest or Ministry to Stand in His Stead.

Therefore, Being True Worshippers, we have a responsibility to make sure that our Offerings, Tithes and Gifts are placed on The Foundation of Righteousness and Holiness. 2 Chronicles 31:4-8.

Nehemiah 10:28-39. The main benefit of Tithing is for The Lord our God to Bless us in all the work of our hands which we should perform. Deuteronomy 14:29.

Malachi 3:10-12. Says:

"Bring ye all the Tithes into the storehouse, that there may be meat in Mine House, and Prove Me now herewith, Saith The Lord of Hosts, if I Will Not Open you the windows of Heaven, and pour you out a Blessing, that there shall not be room enough to receive it. And I Will Rebuke the devourer for your sakes, and he shall not destroy the fruits of your ground; neither shall your vine cast her fruit before the time in the field, Saith The Lord of Hosts. And all nations shall call you Blessed: for ye shall be a delightsome land, Saith The Lord of Hosts".

In other words, God's Continual Favors upon our Lives forever, which also continues to be upon the lives of our Generation to come. We can't live our lives for ourselves, we have to live our lives with the view that we can leave A Spiritual Inheritance that is wrapped up in The Will of God that our Generation will become A Blessing, based on the Foundation of the Sacrifice that we have Started through Tithing; but let me repeat, only those who are True Worshippers can accept the importance of what is being said.

Have you ever wonder to yourself why it is that whatever God Allows The True Worshippers to Perform, it brings forth Blessing and Prosperity, no matter how simple it seems! Then if someone else try to do the same job, it does not bring forth the same results, because the difference is The Favor of God. It must also be noted that according to The Book of Leviticus Chapter 27:30&31. Which says:

"And all the Tithe of the Land, whether of the seed of the land, or of the tree, is The Lord's: it is Holy unto The Lord. And if a man will at all redeem ought of his Tithes, he shall add thereto the fifth part thereof".

This means that if it is that we are face with difficulties, that we must borrow from our Tithes; God's Requirement is then for us to put a fifth part back on that which we have borrowed, meaning 5% of anything we have borrowed, and The Tithes will still be considered Holy and Acceptable for God to Receive it at our hands; but if we borrow The Holy Offering, that belongs to God and do not add the

5% to what we have borrowed, then it will no longer considered to be Holy and Acceptable for God to Receive it for Our Sacrifice / Offering.

A Time For Tithing, it is God's Recommendation in this Message that Believers choose when it is actually the time that we have acknowledge that we are True Worshippers and are Living Holy and Acceptable Lives, then to be in the position that we must know that in order for us to continue Being A Blessing for ourselves and for our Generation to come, then Tithing Is A MUST.

All Honor, Glory and Power Forever and Ever to The Only Living God, Jesus Christ our Soon Coming King. From the Servant of God Pastor Lerone Dinnall.

A Time For Tithing.

Flushing Your Circle, Thus Renewing God's Divine Relationship.

Message # 49

Date Started March 18, 2017
Date Finalized March 20, 2017.

Genesis 12:1-3.

"Now The Lord had said to Abram, Get thee out of thy country, and from thy kindred, and from thy father's house, unto a land that I Will Shew thee: and I Will Make of thee a great nation, and I Will Bless thee, and Make thy name great; and thou shalt be a blessing: And I Will Bless them that bless thee, and Will Curse him that curseth thee: and in thee shall all the Families of the earth be blessed".

Genesis 50:24-25.

"And Joseph said unto his brethren, I die: and God Will Surely Visit you, and Bring you out of this land unto the land which He Sware to Abraham, to Isacc, and to Jacob. And Joseph took an oath of the children of Israel, saying, God Will Surely Visit you, and ye shall carry up my bones from hence.

1 Corinthians 13:11.

"When I was a child, I spake as a child, I understood as a child, I thought as a child: but when I became a man, I put away childish things".

2 Corinthians 6:17&18.

"Wherefore come out from among them, and be ye separate, Saith The Lord, and touch not the unclean thing; and I Will Receive you, and Will Be A Father unto you, and ye shall be My Sons and Daughters, Saith The Lord Almighty".

I Greet The Family of God in none other Name but The Name of Jesus Christ, by which all The Family in Heaven and Earth is Named, which are Destined to be a part of God's Kingdom. Ephesians 3:14&15. Again this is a privilege for me to be in a Position as this, to be an able Instrument for God that I should write, that God's People can have a constant reminder of what is The Requirements of God. I'm also enjoying the experience of being able to Receive Messages from God, and then to write, for the Main purpose being that My Children will be able to benefit from the exposure of these Words of Revelations; that when am not able to, or no longer around, these Words will be A Guideline for My Children, and their Generations to come.

One of the main thing which was identified; why the Children of Israel found themselves in sin and away from God's Favor and Protection, is because at every event, the Training of what a person should observe to remain in God was Ignored, and Forgotten, thus the next Generation found themselves in positions that they knew not God for themselves, nor were they Trained to live in The Fear of God. I'm therefore making it my responsibility, to make sure that I Train My Son and Daughter to make certain that they walk in The Will of The Almighty GOD.

Flushing Your Circle Thus Renewing God's Divine Relationship; the first thing to understand and to bring to the fulfillment of the Minds of God's People, is the Fact that each person we see, whether it be on the road, at work or in Church, that person has a Circle that influence the Atmosphere and the Surroundings in which that person dwells, thus influencing the decisions that are made by that person. And many times it is seen that many persons have chosen wisely who and what becomes a part of their Surrounding, thus influencing the very Atmosphere of that person's life; on the other hand, there are many that have the penetration of Bad Seeds in the very Surroundings of their Circle, thus causing the Atmosphere of their lives to be very unhealthy.

Now, we know for a Fact that not many people there is that will willfully inflict or cause hurt to themselves and to the Surrounding in which they dwell; but the Fact of life is, not everyone is grown to be fully Mature in The Spirit Man, thus many of us even though it is that we have grown Physically, this meaning in body and in stature; the most important part of our growth is yet to be realized which is The Spirit Man, that understands What, When and Why God's Commandments is important, to implement measures to make sure that, that which God Has Instructed, is fulfilled by the actions of this now fully Mature Spiritual Man.

We wonder at times why it is that many unfortunate things happen around our Circle, when the truth to all of this, is the very company that we allow to be a part of our Circle, which then causes The Absence of God's Presence, removing The Barrier of Protection and Circle of God's Favor upon our Lives.

Here is the Truth: God and Sin cannot Mix, and will never Mix, as far as the East is from the West, and The Glory of the Sun in comparison to that of The Glory of the Moon, so is it for God against those who are not walking in The Likeness of His Light; it is said in The Book of Isaiah 59:1-8. Verse 1-4 says:

"Behold, The Lord's Hand is not shortened, that it cannot save; neither His Ear heavy, that it cannot hear: But your iniquities have separated between you and your God, and your sins have hid His Face from you, that He Will Not Hear. For your hands are defiled with blood, and your fingers with iniquity; your lips have spoken lies, your tongue hath muttered perverseness. None calleth for justice, nor any pleadeth for truth: they trust in vanity, and speak lies; they conceive mischief, and bring forth iniquity".

Can any of these actions that are products of the Seed of Envy, Please The Living God, that will Influence His Presence to Dwell amongst those who are surrounded by darkness? And many times we find ourselves in these Company, and have invited these persons in our Circle, and for some strange reason we ask ourselves why was not God Able to Deliver us in that Challenge that we faced. And for this I summit to our understanding that we are Ignorant and still remain yet a child towards The Requirements of that which God Called us to Perform. The Bible made mention of this condition of the Mind for many of God's People which seems to think that Mixing Christianity with Darkness is acceptable in The Eyes of God, in The Book of Romans Chapter 1:28-32. It Says:

"And even as they did not like to retain God in their knowledge, God Gave them over to a reprobate mind, to do those things which are not convenient; being filled with all unrighteousness, fornication, wickedness, covetousness, maliciousness, full of envy, murder, debate, deceit, malignity; whisperers, backbiters, haters of God, despiteful, proud, boasters, inventors of evil things, disobedient to parents, without understanding, covenantbreakers, without natural affection, implacable, unmerciful: who knowing the judgment of God, that they which commit such things are worthy of death, not only do the same, but have pleasure in them that do them".

Now here is the Question that is Hot on the Fire:

"If Our Circle is filled with one of the Categories of what is listed in this Scripture; will the presence of such a person influence the **Now Relationship** We have with The Heavenly Father?

What do you think"! _____. I leave My Readers to Answer that Question.

The Bible Said in The Book of Hosea 4:6.

"My People are destroyed for a lack of knowledge: because thou hast rejected knowledge, I Will Also Reject thee, that thou shalt be no priest to me: seeing thou hast forgotten the law of thy God, I Will Also Forget thy children".

Being Ignorant of what God's Word Command is a Sin, because the Lack of God's Word Brings forth the Manifestation of every type of

Sin; and every type of Bad Company within A Child of God Circle, will reflect and thus creating a big impact of Rejection of God's Presence.

Here is a Fact: Within our personal life, if we can make a listing of the amount of Clothes we have, and shoes we buy for wearing; if we should be truthful to ourselves, and begin to take Inventory of that which we are truly in need of, and is of benefit to our everyday necessity, we will then find that there are many Clothes and Shoes which we now have in possession that are just hanging in the Closet and under the bed that are simply occupying space; because for many of these Clothes and Shoe, they are not even worn by us in a long time.

Now this is the point of this Fact; all these unwanted Clothes and Shoe, although it should be of benefit to us, it now falls in a Category that it remains and cost a Drainage on our pockets, allowing our Finance to suffer the influence of our Lust for wanting more of what will never be of benefit to our Spiritual Walk. So is it with the Circle of our Company, if we should, and let me rephrase: We Must as Christians begin our personal Inventory of our Christian Circle, Family Circle, Work Circle and also Social Circle; to make sure that we begin a Flushing of our Circle, thus removing every and any Company within our Circle that just does not measure up to the Requirements of Allowing for God's Presence to Remain within our Circle.

I don't know about My Readers, but this I do know for Myself: If My Circle only contains The Presence of God, then that's a Circle I can live with. The song writer made mention in his song that Says:

"Jesus first and everything comes after".

When a Child of God have done a proper Inventory of those who are to be involved in his Circle, then it will be realized that many persons who are now Circulating within our Circle, are actually an Enemy of Righteousness, and thus cannot be allowed to remain in our Circle, because we are now Mature Spiritual Man, and know for a Fact, that if those Persons / Influences remain, then we will find ourselves drifting away from The Presence of The Lord. And if we move away from Light, it means we are now in Darkness and Death.

Let me share something with My Readers, coming from The Man of God Bishop Austin Whitfield, as he was Teaching the young people of My Time, about how to identify if a person Truly Loves you. Bishop Whitfield Said, and I Quote:

"If a person truly Loves you, with the intention of wanting to be a part of your life; then that person has to Love your Soul, therefore it must be the responsibility of each young person to make sure that we have identify that such an individual actually Loves our Soul; meaning that if they love your Soul, they will never do anything to endanger our Souls to commit an Act that we Sin against God".

Question: Those who are currently a part of our Circle, what are they Influencing us to do and to Become; are they desiring for us to commit Sin? Wake up! That person, no matter who the person is or what Title they hold in your life, that person Does not care about you, that person does not Love your Soul, that person will never be able to allow your Circle to be healthy that it will Attract The Presence of God, therefore be very careful of that person, and now start to consider the action of Flushing that person from your Circle, but this is only My Advice, the decision is left for My Readers to fulfill. **"Free Will"**.

I know it is the Mindset of many people to think that once they have Flushed their Circle, who then is going to fill the Gap? God's People have got to Elevate their level of thinking to the belief that God Will Always Fill the Gap; God Will Always Provide a way of escape; God Is more than Capable to Fill your now Flushed Circle from every influence of unrighteousness to now fill that same Circle with every Influence of Righteousness, that will allow for His Presence to Continually be in the Generation of The Righteous Seed. And it will be identified that The Promises of God Will Follow the Circle that is filled with Righteousness, which brings forth the evidence that says:

"Then shalt thou call, and The Lord Shall Answer; thou shalt cry, and He Shall Say, Here I Am. If thou take away from the midst of thee the yoke, the putting forth of the finger, and speaking vanity". Isaiah 58:9.

We will never be able to know and to fulfill that which is our true capability in God, unless we have come to the understanding that some people who we would consider to be Friends and Company in this life, are the very people that God Is Asking for us to Flush from our Circle. Imagine this, The Bible Said in The Book of Revelation 19:7&8.

"Let us be glad and rejoice, and Give Honour to Him: for the marriage of The Lamb is come, **and His Wife hath made herself ready**. And to her was granted that she should be arrayed in fine linen, clean and white: for the fine linen is the righteousness of saints".

This is how God Looks on A Child of God that is walking in His Likeness; and if we should check that Child of God Circle, we would identify that it has been Completely Flushed from all Influence of Unrighteousness, to now be in a Position to now be able to wear the Garment that is White and Clean. What if that Child of God then decide to Mix Righteousness with Unrighteousness? Will that person be able to reach A Qualified State that they can now wear the Garment of Righteousness? The Answer is No.

This Scripture also made reference to the Fact that The Wife of The Lamb hath made herself READY. We can never be in a position to reach a State of Readiness if it is that we decide to continue with the Circle that reminds our life of only being A Child. Now that we have become Mature Christians, the Circle of our lives must contain Mature Spiritual Individuals that are willing to make Mature Decisions that will help to Influence The Presence of God rather than cause The Presence of God to Be Far Away from our Circle.

Note: Flushing your Circle is not an easy task, but certainly it is a necessary task; it's going to take a lot of Fasting and Prayers and Reading of God's Word and also personal Reevaluation of our Christian walk to now identify what is important from those who are not important. I'm sure we have heard of a saying that Says:

"Ants follow Fat".

This is true; so is it with those who are aspiring to live A Righteous life for God; we are the Light of the World, a city set on a hill that cannot be hid; we are The Church that is built on the gates of hell, therefore our very presence will bring forth a Transformation in the Elements of Darkness, in a way that Darkness always knows that whenever Light is around, his glory is less attractive; Darkness has also studied The Glory of Light, and have found out that light is and can only be Effective if only that person who represent The Light keeps their Circle unspotted from all the Elements of Darkness; therefore, The Elements of Darkness will always seek to put Traps and Snares in the pathway of Light, under the pretense that these Traps and Snares comes in the likeness of being our very best friends that cares so much about us; which is in fact a Lie; they are set in our Circle to cross the connection of our Relationship that we have worked so hard to develop with our God.

It is identified in The Book of Numbers Chapter 22 through Chapter 24. That Balak the king of Moab desired that a Prophet named Balaam should be called, with the intention of asking Balaam to Curse who God Had Bless, which Represence The Light; this Balaam could not do what king Balak requested, because he was warned by God that he Cannot Curse who God Had Bless. But this Balaam at the end of everything that was done, he gave counsel to the king of Moab, by instructing him in the paths of knowing exactly what to do to cause The Presence God to no longer be with The Children of Israel; by letting the king know that all he had to do, is to allow Israel to sin, by allowing the Daughters and Sons of his land to Married The Children of Israel, and by doing this the Daughters and Sons of Moab will then create change in the hearts of The Children of Israel, to move away from Serving The True and Living God to now kneel down to serve Idols.

This was done by perfect planning, thus causing The Anger of The Lord to Be Poured Out upon The Children of Israel. If The People of God thinks for a minute that the Enemy is not already planning to see how it is that they can Overcome God's People, to inject different type of people in our Circle, that will then influence our decisions to Serve God, to now move to serve Sticks and Stones, Idols, and one of the main god that is in circulation is Money. The enemy would not mind if we hang up our Salvation for the Riches and Fame and Vanities of this World.

Come to think about it, how much do we actually know about the persons who have become a part of Our Circle. I Guarantee that if we do a proper Inventory of Our Circle it will surprise us to see who it is that we are associated with. Some of these persons may be a Gun man, Rapist, Liars, Iniquity workers, Backbiters, Covetous and Envious individuals etc. And all these different types of spirits, brings forth a different type of Attitude in our Circle, which then creates a Blockage from The Presence of God. There is a saying that goes like this:

"Show me your Company and I will tell you who you are".

In Psalms 66:18. The Bible Says:

"If I regard iniquity in my heart, The Lord Will Not Hear me".

The findings of this Message allows me to realize that, I personally may not be at fault, but those who are My Associates may be doing something that is not Pleasing to God, which then stops me from Receiving My Breakthrough or Deliverance from God. And such is the story with Joshua and The Children of Israel, when it is that Achan took the Babylonian Garment, that which was Commanded by God to be Destroyed; he took it, and hid it under his tent, with no one knowing about what he had done, but God Knew; and this event cause The Presence and Favor of God to Be Removed from The Children of Israel even though it was Joshua, God's Servant was leading Israel at that time.

Joshua had to Consult God, and God Revealed to Joshua who it was that caused The Presence and Favor of God to be Removed from the Camp of The Israelites. Joshua Chapter 7.

God Is No Respecter of persons; Ephesians 6:9.

God Is Always Expecting for His People to Know what is Written in THE BIBLE, to thus know how to stay away from all the Traps, Snares and Guise of the Enemy. And many times our Circle is completely filled with the Enemy and we don't know, because we don't know The Words of God to Identify who is our Enemy.

Our Enemies are those who are in Violation of God's Word, and some of the times we find ourselves to Become A Enemy to God, because we are not Doing what His Word Says. And I will Repeat: The Enemy of A Child of God is any and every person that is not walking in accordance to what The Word of God Ask us to walk. Can we just imagine within Our Circle, we are taking advice from those who don't have The Word of God to be their Direction.

Big Problem For Us!

It is important to note that if A Child of God refuse to Flush their Circle, the walk of Holiness will never start; because Holiness Is Separation, thus A Divine Relationship with God Will Never Be Realized.

That's The FACTS!

I Honor, Praise and Glorify The Living GOD, Jesus Christ The Saviour of Mankind. Continue to Pray for My Continual Strength In The Lord, and for this Ministry to always Be Successful. From The Servant of The Lord, Pastor Lerone Dinnall.

Flushing Your Circle, Thus Renewing God's Divine Relationship.

If The Type of Friends or Saints We Associate With Causes Us To Sin; Then It's Time To Change Our Friends or Company.

Message # 56

Date Started August 21, 2017
Date Finalized August 21, 2017.

Greetings in The Mighty Name of Jesus Christ, Happy am I to be writing this another Inspiring Message. Closer than a Brother My Jesus is to me, He's My Dearest Friend in everything I need, He's My Rock, My Shield and Hiding place, closer than a Brother Jesus is to me.

For those of us who are conscious of what we do to ensure that everything we commit to doing is in Resemblance of what The Word of God Demands for us to do, then we are the Chosen Generation that have seen the benefits to walk in The Light of God's Word which brings forth The Manifestation of His Character; therefore, We are completely Mindful of the Fact that to every Action there is indeed a Equal Reaction.

And while it is that many have accustomed their ways that it must be in line to have the commitment and influence of Friends; The Children of God, The Tithes for The Lord have been Born in the Understanding to realize that those who should esteem themselves to resemble the likeness of a Friend are indeed those who have also aligned their will and Character to The Likeness and The Manifestation of The Most High God. Because The Bible Being Our Example and Our Guide for Life Has Illustrated for us the Examples of all those who have walked contrary towards The Will and Commandments of The Most High God. And it is certain, God Ways and Commands will indeed insure that there is a Bright Future for all those who desire to walk after The Commandments of The Most High God.

The word Friend and Saint of God sounds good, but we've got to be very Careful of those who we have accepted in Our Minds to be in Our Circle to represent the likeness of a Friend or a Saint of God. Because the Truth is, those who we have accepted in our Minds has a Friend and as a Child of God, are those who we have allowed our Guards of Protection to be Relaxed; therefore, We are no longer conscious, and our Focus will no longer be at its ultimate best around these persons because Our Mind and spirit would have become so relaxed, that we would think or be born in the belief that there is nothing that this person would do, that will cause us to get hurt. This concept sounds good to the ears, but I think that we are mistaking The Character of The Most High God to the Character of vulnerable men. Men like ourselves who are exposed to the Elements that cause man to Sin.

The World has mistaken who and what a Friend truly is; likewise, The Church has mistaken who and what a True Child of God Must Represent. And it is a Fact that we are daily being fed the corruptible food of the Teachings of the World by Television, Radio, Internet, Telephone, What's App Etc. Many things that we do, if we but only take one step backwards to apply The Word of God to that which we do, then we would have identified that, that which we have done is in complete contradiction to what The Word of God Is Saying. I've learnt so far in My Christian walk, that Personal Salvation is a PATIENT WALK. God's Will and Desire for us is never a Quick Fix; it is rather A Continual Patient Work, like being in The Hands of The Potter. The only difference is that The Work that God Is Doing in our lives, takes a complete lifetime for it to Be Fulfilled. Therefore, For those who think that God Is Only Going to Put a Patch and then let us go, we need to think again.

There must be the Understanding born in God's People to be Knowledgeable that unless those who we would consider to be our Friend or a Saint of God, are actually those who have been Born Again like ourselves. If it is that we are Born Again; then the Fruit of the tree will never lie. A Born Again Friend or Saint Bears The Fruits of The Spirit of God; therefore having Friends or Saints like these in our Circle, is like having a constant reminder that God Is Always Around. On the other hand, if we have not been Born Again, then our Friends and Saints will reflect exactly who we are; because God Is Not Stupid, He Knows those who are Real from those who are only Pretending. And it is The Will of God, that He Has Gathered those who are Real, True Holy Ghost Baptize Believer to be in a Circle by themselves; and it is The Mysteries of God that He Has Created A Screening that sees those who are not yet Born Again, to remain by themselves, to associate with people of their own likeness. There is a clear Fact; that being, that God Will Protect His Tithes, meaning the Tenth of People or Saints that are Stamp with The Mark of Holiness upon their Forehead.

The Topic Says: "If the type of Friends or Saints we associate with causes us to sin, then it's time to change our Friend or Company".

Not everyone will accept this knowledge, because when a man is blind, because God Caused him to Remain Blind, there is nothing that man can do to change his condition; and am not talking about Physical Blindness, rather I'm making reference to the Spiritual Blindness. It is God that Make Changes, it is God that Open the physical eyes to behold the corruption, and it is God that Separates His People from corruption to become The Holiness of God. Everything is Fixed; we are living in the days that it's being revealed before our very eyes, which says: Let The Righteous be righteous still and let the filthy be filthy still.

There is to be found many Stories in The Bible that Reflects exactly what this Topic is making reference to; one of which is the Story to be found in The Book of 2 Samuels Chapter 13:1-19. In summary, David's son Amnon, in his state of mind claimed that he Loved his sister Tamar, who was the direct brother to Absalom, in other words Amnon was the half-brother to Tamar, by sharing the same father but not the same mother; while Absalom and Tamar shared the same Father and Mother. It was found that Amnon Lusted, not Love; he Lusted for the beauty and virginity of his sister Tamar, that the Lust caused him to become as it was a sick man, his spirit became sick because the Lusty desires was not being Fed. Amnon had a friend, in Verse 3-5 it explained what Amnon friend advised him to do.

"But Amnon had a friend, whose name was Jonadab, the son of Shimeah David's brother: and Jonadab was a very **SUBTIL** man. And he said unto him, why art thou, being the king's son, lean from day to day? Wilt thou not tell me? And Amnon said unto him, I love Tamar, my brother Absalom's sister. And Jonadab said unto him, lay thee down on thy bed, and make thyself sick: and when thy father cometh to see thee, say unto him, I pray thee, let my sister Tamar come, and give me meat, and dress the meat in my sight, that I may see it, and eat it at her hand".

The remainder of the Story proved that the influence of Amnon's friend was manifested that a great sin was done in the land of Israel; it also proved that, that which Amnon called Love, was in Fact a Great Lust to have pleasure at the expense of his sister's life. All this took place because of the sin that David himself did, when he took Bathsheba and killed her husband Uriah. A Great Sin which then Births another Great Sin, and continued to birth Sin throughout the life and lineage of king David.

Let's have a look at the Reaction of Sin. David being the king, received the request from his son Amnon, to let his Daughter Tamar prepare for Amnon her Brother a meal; because it was sold in his mind that this was the only way that he could feel better and recover from his sickness. And David being a Wise king; because of the Sin he himself committed could not Discern to understand that this was a trap for his Daughter; he gave the approval, which resulted in Amnon raping his own sister, and then the worst part of the Story is that after he raped her, he wanted nothing to do with her.

It can also be observed that the friends that a person have associated themselves with, is in fact the FIXED Influence that is Given By God unto man, to determined their own Destiny. Then many may ask the Question: "Why is it that I have Friends like these"? The answer is simple; because the friends we have is a complete reflection of the person we Truly are. A Wise person would seek to analyze this theory to be True; and upon accepting the truth of what is said, then to make sure that we analyze our Circle to ensure that the type of Friends or Saints we associate with are those which have A Likeness of God The Almighty. Without this Likeness of God, we are sure to Fail.

King Ahab received a Wife that resembled his Character that ensured that through her Influence upon his life, that his whole life and his Kingdom was FIXED for Destruction from God. And there was nothing he could have done to change the outcome. The Bible Declares that Jezebel, by her Influence of being the king's Wife, Planned, Fixed and also Sealed with the king's Seal the destruction of Naboth, because Naboth refused to sell king Ahab his Vinegard that was left as an Inheritance from his father. This story clearly Manifest that a Good man will receive a Good Wife and Good Friends to remain as a Good Influence towards the Decisions that he should make; and also a Wicked man will receive a Wicked Wife and Wicked Friends to remain in his company to make sure that his simple Decisions is Influenced with Wicked Intentions. Everything is already FIXED from The Foundation of the World.

Let us Pray:

Father of Heaven and Earth, We come before Your Face, knowing that Thou Art The God of Abraham, Isacc and Israel, Thou art also The God of Covenant; Thou art Jesus Christ The Lamb of God. We Ask In The Name of Jesus Christ that You Will Forgive Us of Past Sins, Present Sins and also Future Sins. Father we have Identified through this Message that Your Presence is of Great Importance to our Development and Existence; Father we Pray that You Will Open our Spiritual eyes that we will be able to guard our Souls from every Influence that is not of Your Will Being Done in our Lives to Obtain Heaven. Father we Pray for True Friends and True Saints to be in the Environment that we Live and Worship, that we will continue to be Influenced to Grow in Your Grace to Become The Mature Spiritual

Trust No One That Does Not Have The Appetite To Serve God.

Message # 45

Date Started June 6, 2017
Date Finalized June 17, 2017.

Father of Heaven in The Name of Jesus Christ, I call upon You to Send forth an Anointing through this Message, that whosoever will come in contact with this Message being A True Worshipper, that You Will Allow their eyes to be open to every possibilities of the Plans and Devices of the Enemies; that those who are Born of The Spirit of God, will have the Eyes of The Lord to Identify the hidden secrets that are planned daily by those who esteem themselves to be and to become our friends; also Lord I Pray that You Will Grant unto us Your True Worshippers, The Divine Intelligence to deal with those who are even a part of our Circle being family by Natural Birth and not of Spiritual Birth; Lord, in The Name of Jesus Christ, The Lamb of God I also pray that You Will Grant unto us Your Servants, The Divine Wisdom to Associate with those who are in The Church, those who only have a disguise of Righteousness, but inwardly they are the angel of darkness; open our Minds Dear Lord, that we will not be Ignorant of the devices of the enemy, because there are many; let this Message Stand as a Pillar of Righteousness for all times, that Your People will be Anointed by these words, I Pray only in The Name of Jesus Christ, that Your Will Be Accomplished in the lives of Your People, Amen.

I Honour The Almighty Father in none other Name but The Name of Jesus Christ; Privilege and Blessed am I to be writing this another Inspired Message from God The Father. Many are given a Platform or an Altar to speak on God's behalf, but I Thank God for this privilege of writing, that I can wake up in the middle of the night and type exactly what I have seen in Vision by what has been Revealed to me by The Father Above. In every pattern and direction of life, God Has His Instruments, to Use us in the manner in which He Sees Best; to God Be The Glory, Great Things He Has Done. We will start this Message by looking on some Scriptures in The Bible, to seek to understand what The Lord Would Have for us to Understand.

1 Peter 1:22-25.

"Seeing ye have purified your souls in obeying in the truth through The Spirit unto unfeigned love of the brethren, see that ye love one another with a pure heart fervently: Being Born Again, not of corruptible seed, but of incorruptible, by The Word of God, which Liveth and Abideth Forever. For all flesh is as grass, and all the glory of man as the flower of grass. The grass withereth, and the flower thereof falleth away: But The Word of The Lord Endureth Forever. And this is the word which by the gospel is preached unto you".

To simplify the words that says, Being Born Again means that this individual's life has now move from a point of being consciously dead, to that of being consciously Alive to every Righteous Act. Therefore, The Righteous Seed that is planted and is watered, now seeks to manifest at all times the action of Righteous living.

Galatians 4:28-31.

"Now we, brethren, as Isaac was, are the children of promise. But as then he that was born after the flesh persecuted him that was born after the Spirit, even so it is now. Nevertheless what saith the scripture? Cast out the bondwoman and her son: for the son of the bondwoman shall not be heir with the son of the freewoman. So then, brethren, we are not children of the bondwoman, but of the free".

There is always Hard Decisions to be made for the life of A Child of God; and one of those Decisions is an earnest desire for The Spirit of God in us to be Separated from everything and everyone that would seek to destroy the life of The Temple of God. There is a True Fact of life, and it is that wherever light is, darkness will fail to exist. Therefore, If A Child of God is surrounded by an environment of Darkness, then the Question must be asked; are we then The Light of the World, A City set upon a hill that cannot be hid? And this is the Big Question: If that Child of God then identify that they are surrounded by darkness; why is it that there is still the Appetite to remain in the Circle or Company of which we now find ourselves to be in?

1 John 3:1-10.

"Behold, what manner of love the Father hath bestowed upon us, that we should be called the sons of God: therefore the world knoweth us not, because it knew Him not. Beloved, now are we the sons of God, and it doth not yet appear what we shall be: but we know that, when He Shall Appear, we shall be like Him; for we shall see Him as He Is. And every man that hath this hope in him purifieth himself, even as He Is Pure. Whosoever committeth sin transgresseth also the law: for sin is the transgression of the law. And ye know that He Was Manifested to Take Away our sins; and in Him is no sin. Whosoever Abideth in Him sinneth not: whosoever sinneth hath not seen Him, neither known Him. Little children, let no man deceive you: he that doeth righteousness is righteous, even as He Is Righteous. He that committeth sin is of the devil; for the devil sinneth from the beginning. For this purpose The Son of God Was Manifested, that He Might Destroy the works of the devil. Whosoever is Born of God doth not commit sin; for His Seed Remaineth in him: and he cannot sin, because he is Born of God. In this the children of God are manifest, and the children of the devil: whosoever doeth not righteousness is not of God, neither he that loveth not his brother".

Now here is a part of The Message that will be very Interested. The words that Says:

"Whosoever is Born of God doth not commit sin".

Now for many years and in many Sunday School I heard this Topic being mentioned, but was still not satisfy with the explanations of what was being expressed. Now the first thing that any and every Child of God can express, if we are Truthful, is the fact that we have sinned, and the fact that in the future we will and would have made some mistakes that causes us to sin. But reading The Bible, it clearly says, not once, but twice:

"He that Abideth and is Born of God Sinneth not".

Which then leaves us in a condition of Mind to wonder and to analyze whether or not we are truly Saved? But after considering what The Word of God Is Saying, I Asked The Lord to Explain the meaning of this parable; and the Answer never came to me at the same time, but after thinking about it for a few days, and Asking The Lord again what it means, the Response came to me like a flood. The Lord Said:

"Can that which is already paid for, have anymore need for it to be paid for again"?

The Lord Continued to Explain that, The Death He Died on Calvary's Cross was not for A Generation or A Dispensation, but was in Fact for All Generations and All Dispensations, for All Times and All Seasons. Therefore, The Lord Says that this Sacrifice was for A Clothing / A Complete Atonement, that was offered once and for all those who will accept the Belief that Jesus Christ Is The Lamb of God which taketh away the Sins of the World. Therefore those who will believe, even though there is the Fact that they have sinned; because of the belief in Jesus Christ The Lamb of God; that sin of the Past, Present and Future would have been washed away.

Now before we came to God and Believed; God Knew about the sin of our Past; Present and Future; and He Accepts us, just has we are; but this is the condition; God Accepts us with all these faults, to wash away and Bury these faults forever, with the now expectation that we will identify who we were, to now seek to transform by The Seed of His Spirit to Become who God Needs us to Become.

The Lord Reveals that becoming Born Again starts with that individual Truly Repenting of the Sins they have committed, therefore even though there will be mistakes in the future, the Attitude of Repentance still remains, that there is a continual desire for that Child of God to Repent to meet The Perfect Man of Being Born Again. The Lord Reveals that, there is five (5) different Stages and Levels to a person Becoming Truly Born Again.

> Stage One: There are those that are at a Level in their lives that they are only a Believer of The Revelation of Jesus Christ.

> Stage Two: There are those that have moved from the Level of being A Believer of Jesus Christ to now become A Repented Baptized Believer. (Disciple).

> Stage Three: There are those who continue from the previous Levels, and now have Received The Seed of The Holy Ghost, which is The Living Conscience of God.

> Stage Four: There are those who are not satisfy with just Receiving The Seed of The Holy Ghost, and are now desirous of Becoming Filled with The Holy Ghost. This is realized when it is identified by such a person that even though they have Received The Holy Ghost; there is still some fruits of The Spirit that have not yet given Birth in their lives.

> Stage Five: You would think that after your filled, that, that would be it; but there is still the Level that only a few will accept to reach being The Tithes of Saints for God, which identify those who are Born Again, and that Level is to now become Full Up of The Holy Ghost; now after A Child of God is Full Up of The Holy Ghost, then that's the time that you're considered to be fully Born Again; which means that you're so Full of God, that there is absolutely no space left for anything else to occupy; which means that A Born Again according to God's Description, Cannot Sin, there is no space and appetite for that person to sin, because God Has Now Full Every Crease, Corners and Cracks of that person whole Mind, Body and Soul.

Yes, I know that there are many Teachings and Preaching that suggest that the moment that we Believe and Baptize, is the very moment we are Born Again; but that's not what God Revealed. There are many that are covered under the cloak of their own belief and Man's Teaching, that all it takes is to just Believe, or just Baptize; or to confess with our mouth that we believe in The Lord Jesus Christ, when the Truth is, that's only one or two level of what is truly Required. Belief without the continual action on the pathway of that belief is no belief; but rather that's only the belief of the mouth for that moment.

Did we really believe that to Inherit Heaven was going to be as easy as to just say we believe, and do an action of Baptism? It is The Continuation of the Belief that makes the Belief Effective; believing for one part of our lives and then not having the focus to do what it take to continue the actions of that belief, is not considered Faithful in The Eyes of God. To Become Truly Saved, is to Be Born Again; we are not Truly Saved until we have reached the Climax of Becoming Full Up of The Holy Ghost; then we will find the evidence that every speech, every movements, every decisions, every person we associate with, is in fact, and has Become A Circle of Baptized Holy Ghost Full Believers.

Many of us has started the journey of Holiness to Become Saved; some are at a higher Level than some; but it will be fully realized when we have been Full of The Holy Ghost, that this is the time that we are Born Again; this however will take time for A Child of God to reach in order to Become Born Again / Full Up of The Holy Ghost.

This Revelation By God Have Demonstrated to me, and should also demonstrate to us, that even though there is found in The Church one (100) or two (200) hundred members; there is the clear fact, according to The Revelations of God that the reason why there is still a lot of mistake still occurring in The House of God, is because even now at present, there is still just A Tithes of Saints that have obtained The Exclusive Level of Being Born Again / Full Up of The Holy Ghost.

And even now at present there is found in The Church A Mixed Multitude; some are at a Level of just Being A Believer, some are at a Level that they have just found out what it is to be in a Position that they have Repented; some Saint are in The Church that have only Received The Holy Ghost, others have Experienced Being Filled with The Holy Ghost; and there are those that have Eclipse The Level of Being Filled, to now Experiencing and Living a life that they are now

Full Up of The Holy Ghost / Born Again; and it must also be noted that there are also those that are in The Church to Spy Out The Liberty of The Saints of God; meaning, they are not a Believer, they have not Repented, they have not Received The Holy Ghost, they are not Filled with The Holy Ghost, and it also means that they are not Full Up of The Holy Ghost which means Born Again.

Therefore, When we have in The Church the different Levels of Minds which brings forth the different Operations of different spirits, "Divisions", which is not of The Spirit of God; then we can understand the confusions that takes place within The House of God. We may wonder at times why it is that there are some in The Church, that after they have reached a certain Level in God, that no matter what anyone try to do to them, it doesn't shake them, because they are so Full of The Spirit of God that there is no longer any more space for anything anymore to affect them.

And these are the persons that when they are Full Up of The Holy Ghost / Born Again; these persons are Selected by God to move out of the common congregation to now be set by themselves to Birth A Work for God at A New Location; because God Uses Born Again, Holy Ghost Full Vessels to Establish The Work that will Stand, and The Work that will stand cannot be Poured into Old Bottles, or else the Bottle will break. Another word for those who are Born Again, Holy Ghost Full, is a word that is used in The Bible as Lively Stones, which are used to Build A Spiritual House.

Here is a Fact that is sad to mention, those who are in The Church that have not yet Become Lively Stones / Full of The Holy Ghost / Born Again; these Saint cannot be used to Become Pillars of Righteousness for The Building of God's Spiritual House, and that's the Truth, the whole Truth and nothing but the Truth.

There are still many of God's People that are confused about who exactly is to be a part of the Circle of their lives, being now A Child of God. And while this still remains to be the Main Puzzle for our lives; the opportunity to elevate in The Mysteries of The Spirit of God past us by; because we are yet to come to the conclusion that, it is not everyone we see and meet, or even associate with in Church, are the ones that The Lord Would Give us Permission to Associate ourselves with.

Here is a thought that keeps springing up in our Heads:

"I can allow that person to become saved".

Truth be told, you and I cannot save not even an Ants.

"We have heard a joyful sound, Jesus Saves, Jesus Saves; spread the news all around, Jesus Saves, Jesus Saves".

Here is My Question: Why is it that we think that the medium through which we got Saved; it will take a completely different or easier experience for someone else to obtain Salvation? One of the number one Requirement for A Child of God to Receive Salvation, is for that person to Experience what it is like to REPENT; even before Baptism, and for some strange reason we believe that it is OK for one person to repent, but then condition changes when it comes on to other people to Receive Salvation. WOW! And this is one of the main Ingredience for disaster, why it is that many Christians that have truly Repented, now finds themselves in the company of so called Believers that knows nothing about what it even takes for a person to Repent; that they can be Qualified for Baptism, and then seek to Receive The Gift of The Holy Ghost.

Then we wonder, how is it that we are surrounded by Christians, and every Decisions we make, turns out that we are Displeasing The Heavenly Father; How can God Be Pleased with a mixture of Light and Darkness, when He Said if we are Lukewarm He Will Spew us out of His Mouth. Each Circle that a person builds around them, is the same Circle of people that Influence each Decisions that we make; think about that!

So, how do we has True Repented and Holy Ghost Filled / Full Christians, Identify those who are not fully persuaded? The Lord Said that we must take heed and beware of the Leaven of the Pharisees and of the Sadducees. St Matthew Chapter 16:6. And St Matthew Chapter 7:15-20.

"Beware of false prophets, which come to you in sheep's clothing, but inwardly they are ravening wolves. Ye shall know them by their fruits. Do men gather grapes of thorns, or figs of thistles? Even so every good tree bringeth forth good fruit; but a corrupt tree bringeth forth evil fruit. A good tree cannot bring forth evil fruit, neither can a corrupt tree bring forth good fruit. Every tree that bringeth not forth good fruit is hewn down, and cast into the fire. Wherefore by their fruits ye shall know them".

What The Word Would Have us to Understand, is that we need to Exercise The Spirit of Patience, especially when it comes on to bringing Individuals in Our Circle; we've got to make sure that we are sure, that such a person is indeed Born of The Spirit of God. One of the number one Purpose of The Holy Ghost is to Protect The Temple of God; therefore we should allow The Spirit of God to Identify who it is that should be Involved in Our Circle. And because the enemy is the Master of Disguise, we need to make sure that each Decisions for who gets Entertained in Our Circle, be done after that Child of God Has Completed a series of Fastings and Prayers, to ask God to Intervene in every Decisions that is to be made, because we only get one shot at Salvation, one shot at life; therefore we cannot afford to make any serious mistakes, especially those we've been warned about.

The Topic Says: "Trust no one that does not have the appetite to serve God". It does not mean that we should not Associate or talk with others; but rather the Topic is allowing us to take a closer look upon those who we come in contact with, that we may seek to Identify those who are Born of God, and if not yet Born Again, then those that are on the channel to Become Born Again. I have A Testimony coming from The Wife of Bishop Austin Whitfield; Mrs. Lady Whitfield, and she Says:

"Hold everyone at Arm's length; and those things that we truly consider that we love, make sure that we hold them with a loose grip; because when the challenge of time comes, and they will come, and change is necessary, that directions of life cross road puzzle must be made, then we will realize that, that which we hold dearest to our hearts, also have an expiration time that it must also go; and if it is that we have made such a firm grip on those things, then when it is time for those things to depart, what will happen, is that it will take us along with it. Life is full of changes, therefore A Child of God must accustom their lives for a lifetime of changes".

I Hope this Testimony helped someone. This Message is not to say that those who are True Christians are those who will never make mistakes, but rather to identify the use and the need of having True Holy Ghost Filled, Baptized Believers around Our Circle.

Bishop Austin Whitfield Would often Say:

"Do not let the words, If I had only know, catch you; you should try your best to know, because the greatest thing in a Man's life is to know; because if you don't know, then you are a fool to what you don't know, and when we find ourselves in the Attitude of not knowing, then we leave ourselves open to every possibilities to get harm from those things which we know not about".

One of the Main Secrets of life is to Understand that to every person there is a spirit or spirits, which brings forth an Influence for that spirit or spirits that occupies their vessel. Now to every manifestation of spirits, there is a Foundation spirit which give birth to every type of spirits that now exist and will exist, and that Foundation spirit is the spirit of Envy, that consumed Lucifer, which also consume the Mind of Eve and then Adam to be fueled by its Influence to believe that, that which they lusted for was indeed possible for possession.

Now it is important for every Child of God to be extremely careful of those who are given permission by us to be a part of our Circle, because with those persons comes also their Individual spirits; and with their manifestation of their spirit which is not of God, comes along with it the Influence of that spirit. Now Influence Children of God, should not be taken lightly; through the Influence of unsaved, A Child of God will be led to sit at the Table of the devil, and are not fully aware that they are under the Influence to offer Sacrifice that are offered to devils. Influence allows sinners that are not customarily a part of our Circle to now creep into be a part of our Circle which is design for us and God.

Therefore to kill the effects of negative Influence, A Child of God have got to Screen everyone that is in constant access to become a part of their Circle. Because Influence cannot be taken for granted;

Influence finds a weakness or crack in each Child of God's Amour of Protection. The Bible States that a Man's gift makes room for him; that is speaking about a Man's Influence that he will obtain after he has given that gift; which then grants unto that man the Power of Influence to change things according to his desires. The Bible and other Books made mention of the Fact that when Lucifer was cast out of Heaven, his Tail drew the third part of Heaven with him; that Tail is making reference to the Influence that Lucifer had Acquired over the Angels.

Therefore, If A Child of God thinks that they can have as many people that don't have the Appetite to Serve God around them, and this action will have no effect on the Influence that these people with these spirit have over their lives; then that Child of God need to think again. Each Decisions that A Child of God makes, it derives from an Influence of the spirit that is in them, or the Influence from the spirit of the people that are directly in their Circle.

This therefore means that each Child of God has got to make sure that when it is time for them to make decisions; be completely certain that all your Decisions is in accordance with The Word of God, and if there will be any Influence from anyone, make certain also that their Decisions is also Influence by The Spirit of God. Any Decisions that is made outside of The Influence of God, then that Child of God will suffer the consequence of those Decisions that are made.

I Hope this Message has been an Inspiration to the lives of The Sons of God; I Give Honour, Glory and offer Praise to The Only Living God, Jesus Christ The Lamb of God. Continue to Pray for The Strength of this Ministry that The Lord's Favor Will Abundantly Rest Upon us, That We'll Be Able to Explore Higher Highs and Deeper Levels in God. From The Servant of God Pastor Lerone Dinnall.

Trust No One That Does Not Have
The Appetite To Serve God.
Be Warned!

STOP Allowing The World To Influence The Church!

Message # 26

Date Started September 12, 2016.
Date Finalized October 6, 2016.

Greetings Family of God in The Wonderful Matchless Name of Jesus Christ our Soon Coming King, how good and pleasant it is for brethren to dwell together in Unity. Happy am I for this Message that God Has Inspired for me to write.

Stop Allowing the World to Influence The Church!

What does that mean?

What is this Message saying, and Asking us to perform?

The first word we should be looking on is the word STOP; which according to The Webster's Dictionary Means:

To cease from or discontinue; I especially like this explanation: To cut off, to restrain or prevent. The word stop, is a VERB, which means that it requires ACTION.

Being A Child of God, a person have got to decide for themselves if they are indeed A Servant of God firstly, before we can associate with a group of people to come together to call ourselves A Church. Let us establish this Fact: A Church is considered to be a group of people, ranging from one upwards, whose belief is in God, and their influence and decisions comes from God. Now if The INFLUENCE and DIRECTION of A Church is not coming from God; then, can we actually call that assembly A Church? If the whole purpose and direction of The Church, is to do what the World is doing or have already done; and to move in the direction that the World wants them to move in; can that Church ever find themselves ready for The Coming of The Lord? The Answer is NO.

The Bible Clearly Speaks to us in The Book of 1 John 2:15-17.

"Love not the world, neither the things that are in the world. If a man love the world, the love of The Father is not in him".

Question: If The Church, which is said to be The Bride of Christ, if what we call The Church; is actually looking like the World; walking like the World; speaking like the World; becoming like the World; then, what we acknowledge to be The Church, is it actually The Waiting Bride that The Lord Is Coming Back For!

I have heard recently, a program on the radio, a survey was done by asking individuals about the Rapture of the Saints; what would they do if they woke up on a certain day, and realized that The Church was gone? It was surprising to know that the host of the program made mentioned that there was an answer he got, that he had to make his listeners hear; not to show that The Church has no meaning; but to show to The Church that if your indeed The Church, we have got to Represent God and not man. The Host said that, one of the response he got, expressed by an individual Was:

"If the Rapture came, they wouldn't know the difference, because all The Churches in their community, is doing the same things that the sinners are doing; therefore, They don't believe that there will be a Rapture for them".

I have seen for myself, and this is not a person's testimony or observation; I've noticed that the order for the day in many Churches, is a word that is called Compromise. This saying is often time used; let God Do The Fixing of The Church. When the fact still remains, that we that are in The Church, keep doing the same things over and over again, thus enabling The Church to be going in a Circle, that we keep making the same mistakes over and over again. Not considering this Fact, that from the beginning of time, God Uses His Servants to Accomplish; Fulfill and Maintain the

Integrity of what The Lord's Directions should be, and not what we think it should be; but to become zealous to follow the Commands that Says:

"LET THY WILL BE DONE ON EARTH HAS IT IS IN HEAVEN".

Being God's Tool does not mean that we are kept in Reservation, but it means that we are active at every second to perform the Duties of that which God Ask us to Accomplish. I am reminded of a saying that The Man of God, Bishop Austin Whitfield usually spoke, and he Says:

"Understanding is a very important Factor in the life of A Child of God; Because he has encountered a lot of Christians, that are told to do what The Lord Expects of them to do, and still they came up with some lame excuse, by saying The Lord Understands why I am not able to perform that which I should do; in an anticipation that The Lord Will Accept whatever they are doing without His Requirements Being Done; The Man of God, would reply to them in this fashion: Yes, of a Truth, The Lord Knoweth them that are His; The Lord Already Knows those that are called to Life Everlasting, and He Also Knoweth them, that are both called and chosen for Damnation".

I think it's a good time to ask ourselves this Question: What am I Called and Chosen to fulfill, that I may be able to inherit my Everlasting Destiny?

There is a Destiny of Everlasting PEACE and JOY; and there is also a Destiny for Everlasting Punishment and Torments; you choose.

There is Seven (7) special Fact, that follows those of us who are determine to be The Light of God in this broken World; we are determined to lift up a standard, that the World may know that the light in us, is going to remain being a Light for God, and will not be influence to change into something that we are not, or what the World need us to become; and this is it:

1. We are so Transparent, that everyone who sees what we are doing, can identify a Relationship in us that comes from God.
2. Our Behavior or Characteristics is completely different from that of Darkness.

3. Whenever anyone looks on us, it's a comparison to that of looking on a Hill or Mountain; a Light House; a Star that shines in the sky; and if we should ever reached the level, which goes beyond all levels, it can be a comparison of someone trying to look in the very Sun, to see if they can understand the nature of why the Sun is so Bright. And yet, the Appearance of The King of kings, will out shine that of the Sun.

4. The Favor of God that Shines over our life, and upon everything that we put our hands to; will reflect The Blessings that only comes from God. There is something significant about The Blessings that Comes from God; there is absolutely nothing that anyone will ever give to us as a gift in this life that can even attempt to measure up to one gift that God Gives to an individual.

5. The Favor of God, or the Light that Shines in us, will not only last for a season of our life; but will outlive our lives, and spread towards our Children, and also our Children's, children. There is no one that calls upon The Name of The Living God, to lift up a standard for Him, can ever be ashamed of the rewards that follows from Serving The Living God. David Says:

    "I have been young, and now am old; yet have I not seen the Righteous forsaken, nor his seed begging bread". Psalms 37:25.

6. And when we and our Generation have finished the time on earth, that is given for us to enjoy the Abundant Life; then, it's time to transform from that which is Physical and Temporal, to discover the Life which has NO ENDING; a life with God, free from all pain; all burden of this vain life; free from all the bills that we encounter every month; free from all sickness; free from temptations and the Devil himself, and also free from DEATH, completely free from Hell and Destructions.

7. The only other thing to expect after all these Blessings, that those who look on us have discovered, is the fact that we are

set for ETERNAL REST. Which will be envied by the devil himself, because we are set to receive a great blessing that he can no longer achieve, because his place is seen no more.

Have we ever asked ourselves this Question! Why is it that the World is so determined, to transform The Church to do what the World is doing? It's simple, the devil control the activities of the World, therefore, If he can just get one foot of influence in The Church, what will stop him from putting another foot in The Church. And if both feet are in The Church; is The Church anymore doing what The Lord Has for The Church to Accomplish; is The Church anymore The Light of the World? If The Church is said to be Light; then the World is said to be Darkness.

Is it not said in The Scriptures:

"A little leaven leaveneth the whole lump". Galatians 5:9.

I speak by experience; all it takes for A Church Family to be spoiled, is for someone, especially if that person in The Church is in a role to command; if this person lower The Standards of God; to call evil good, and good evil; a person that put darkness for light, and light for darkness; a person that calls bitter sweet, and sweet for bitter! Isaiah 5:20. All it takes to destroy A Light House is one act of Compromise, which will result and show the difference from A Church of Believers, to an assembly of people.

Bishop Whitfield would often lament, when he saw for himself the diluting of The Gospel of Christ, He Would Say:

"I'm worried of what I'm seeing, that is happening in The Church; I wonder if Peter; Paul; James and John should look on The Church now; will they be convinced, that The Church of our generation, is it a resemblance of the Foundation they started on the day of Pentecost. Or will they say like Paul, when he visited the Church at Ephesus; Have ye received The Holy Ghost since ye believed"?

Paul came to Ephesus, and saw certain believers attempting to worship, but realized that there was something missing from the worship, which is SPIRIT and TRUTH. Bishop Whitfield was worried then, when he was still strong to do God's Work; what would he say now, if he was still on the earth to observe what we the members of The Church Family Call Serving God; would He be saying yes, this is The Foundation, that The Lord Gave to The Apostles, or would He Say:

"Wi Nuh Ready Yet".

Being The Church can never mean that we are going to please ourselves and please others, or be influence by others to do what God Does Not Need Us To Do. It must be that we have accepted the responsibilities of being A Light House, which makes us A Church; we must Respect the position that God Has Placed us in; and we should be fully Determined to fulfill all the Requirements that The Lord Would Have Us To Fulfill.

There is one main evil that I have discovered growing in The Church, and that evil and wicked device is known to be MONEY or the INFLUENCE OF MONEY. As Leaders and being the main Example in The Church, we know for a fact, that if the Offering that is being offered to God Is Not Clean, then that offering is considered to be polluted, therefore, It will not be Accepted by God. The story of Cain and Abel should be our main example; they both were of the same parents, but one brother had a great consideration of what was worthy to offer to God with respect; while the other brother did not have that respect.

This have I seen with my own eyes; there are members in The Church, that have not learnt God, or they are purposed to do something wrong; that member, while the Sacrifice is being offered, decides to make a phone call or to send a text message in The Church; or to light a cigarette in The House of God; or decides to chew a gum or eat food; they have decided that it is OK to turn The House of God in their personal shop, to sell someone of their goods in The Church of God while the Sacrifice is being offered. The leaders or those in command of the service, turn a blind eye, or just don't say anything; they are of the conclusion, that God Will Fix The Church Himself; not realizing that God Has Put a person in the position to Lead His Church, to lift up a Standard for Him, that the World may see and observe, and learn to respect and appreciate the standards that must be carried out in The House of God.

Did not Jesus Christ Went in The Temple and saw the people selling and buying and also exchanging money in The House of God; The Bible Said that he turned over the tables and ran them out of The Temple; Saying:

"My House shall be called an House of Prayer, but he have made it a den for thieves".

There are some of us that are influence to lower God's Standard because we believe that if we say anything, that would be the last day, that person attends The Church; therefore, Resulting in a lower collecting of the Offerings and Tithes that should be collected on that day.

WHO CARES IF THEY DON'T WANT TO COME BACK!

The Standard should be GOD and not man. Our influence to Serve God should never be driven by money or recognition, but by desiring to fulfill what God Would Have Us To Do. We need to get away from the principle that we believe that it is money or man's support that cause The Church to Survive. Man did not call A Servant of God to do a work for God's Ministry; Money should never be our influence; that because of money, we become afraid to lead The Church of The Living God in the right direction. We should always remember that The Lord Says:

"Upon this Rock I Will Build My Church, and the gate of hell shall not prevail against it".

Once we find ourselves building on The True Foundation, there is absolutely no way we can Fail. I've found myself in situations choosing to confront certain individuals about what is expected of them to Perform for God; their response was more to remind me that they are a Tithes payer, or that they give offering regular; which of the two, speaks nothing towards the Holiness of God.

Can you guess what I said!

I told them to stop paying the Tithes and Offering, and start A New Diet by starting to live A Holy Life for The Lord; because if we spend a lifetime paying our Tithes and Offerings and forget about The HOLINESS, then our lives would be in vain.

Note: Tithes is not paid but rather it is Given Freely.

It's time for us as Preachers; Teachers; Ministers; Missionaries; Evangelist, Pastors and Bishops; It's time for us to destroy the Power and the Influence of MONEY in The Church, because many people use money as a scape goat, or free ticket, to sit down in The Church and cause The Church to be like them, instead of them becoming like God. I'm not here to say that money is not important; no that's not what I'm saying; I'm rather revealing to us a secret that not a lot of people have discovered. It is far better, if there is in The Church, ten (10) members that are living A Holy Life for The Lord, than to have Two Hundred (200) members, that knows nothing about Holiness.

That Ten (10) members, that are living Holy unto God; their Tithes and Offering will benefit The Church a whole lot better, than that which Two (200) members give to The Church, that are not living Holy Lives. And because these people that are not Holy; they are allowed to remain in The Church, because of their Tithes and Offerings; these people now become Dictators to The Ministry of Jesus Christ, therefore having a BIG INFLUENCE on how The Church of God must be directed.

FACT: Everyone that is Truly Saved by God; everything that they do, will Represent God; even the Offering and the Tithes they contribute must be A BLESSING; don't be envious of the Offerings that GOD Did Not Give us for The Church; because if God Didn't Give it, then it's not A Blessing.

Can we just imagine; a person who has not Received The Holy Ghost, has an influence in The Church as to who should conduct A Supper Service; A Fasting meeting or A Prayer meeting; having the influence because of their money, to make request that their son be given the chance to do A Sunday School Message; who has never been in A Bible Class to receive the training of who God Is; or have never receive of the True Spirit of God. These are persons that secretly and quietly; plants a right hand of influence in The Church that seeks only to please their own selfish will and desires. This is the

World's influence that comes in The Church, and let us believe that there is nothing wrong in decorating ourselves with jewelry; there is nothing wrong if we keep our boyfriend and our girlfriend; God Understands. There is nothing wrong in being Married, and divorce to marry another; there is nothing wrong if we have sex before we get married, and to have our children out of Wed Lock; there is nothing wrong if I colour my hair to look like the dance hall queen in The House of God; there is nothing wrong if we have a concert, and invite ungodly men to entertain us; just as long as, at the end of the day, the offering receptacle and The Church Account is filled with cash; there is nothing wrong, because all other Churches are doing it; therefore we can do it too. I leave My Readers to be the Judge, is there something WRONG? _____.

Concerning that of Jewelry; have we ever read in The Bible, that The People of God Decorated themselves with jewelry to enter into Worship before God? We confess that we are following The Bible and The Lord's Commandment; but the more we read it seems to be, that it's the more we choose to do our own will and desire. Take for example, The Bible described The Bride of Christ, The Lamb's Wife, has being granted that she should be arrayed in Fine Linen, Clean and White: for the Fine Linen is the Righteousness of Saints. Revelations 19:6-10. Is there anywhere in this Scripture or in other Scriptures that says that The Bride or the Wife of Christ is arrayed in Jewelries; in earrings; in Chains; in Nose rings; in bangles; in tattoos and other piercings? Search for yourself and then judge for yourself. If you search the Scriptures, you will identify that Jacob before he went back to Bethel to Worship, by the Command of God, he and his Family had great Respect for The House of God; Jacob told his household to put away the strange gods from among themselves; with this being asked, they gave to him all their strange gods, and also their earrings; of which he took them all and buried them under the oak which was by Shechem. Genesis 35:1-5.

This is an example of complete Respect for God and for God's House. This is My Question: If we are indeed The Bride of Christ, and are comfortable with all the Decorations and Distractions; why did not The Bible Make Mention of the custom of what we are now, to prove to ourselves that we are on the right track of becoming The Bride of Christ just as we are! If we do not take this correction, but insist that we are going to do what pleases our own will; then, are we going to ever become The Lamb's Wife, dressed in Fine Linen, White and Clean? The answer is No.

I know that I'm not going to be everyone's favorite Speaker or Pastor, but My focus is not to receive Commendation from man, but rather to Please THE LIVING GOD; My focus is to help some brother and sister to observe a brighter light. Look at this for a minute; what would we say if one day we saw every man that is called to be a Preacher; Pastor; Minister or Bishop; we observed with our eyes that they are arrayed in Earrings; Chains; Bracelets; Nose rings; Shaved eye brows etc. What would the members of The Church now say? Would they say that it is ok, because the women are doing it, therefore, The men can do it as well! Just think and examine it for a moment.

If God Looks on all of us as being Sons of God, whether we be male or female; if we should go by what we have declared to be God's Standard, by saying that it is ok to have the decorations on our bodies to enter into Worship or even to become The Living Sacrifice; then if it is ok for the decorations to be on the women; then, should it not be ok to be on the men, because we are indeed all Sons of God! What goes for the woman; does it not apply also to the man?

Did The Lord Command Adam only, not to eat of the fruits of the tree? That Commandment did not only applied to Adam, but it was also applied to Eve being the woman. Therefore, What goes for the man, goes also for the woman; therefore, If our Revelation of God tells us that decorating ourselves is ok for the woman; then nothing is wrong for the man to do it also! You be the Judge.

Is it that wrong is spelt different for a man than for a woman? Is it that when a man does something right it is Recognized by God; but when a woman does something right it is not Recognized by God? Is THE JUSTIFIED GOD a Compromising God? The Bible Said that The Lord Will Judge with EQUITY, meaning Equal Rights. The Bible

Explains to us in The Book of Revelation Chapter 20:11-15. A part of it Says:

"And I saw the dead, small and great, stand before God; and The Books were opened: and another Book was opened, which is The Book of Life: and the dead were judged out of those things which were written in The Books, according to their works".

I made mention of this Scripture to bring to remembrance that all mankind will be judged; young and old; rich and poor; good and bad; whether you believe or you don't believe; every man's work will be manifested by God Almighty. I'm reminded of a Scripture in The Book of Joshua Chapter 7. In order for Israel to Recommit themselves to God, they had to get rid of sin completely; not partially or to even put a covering over it; they had to do a complete work or else God Would No Longer Stand Up for them. Maybe this was what Jacob observed concerning entering The House of God with strange gods; therefore, He got rid of all the strange gods, before approaching The True and Living GOD.

Not only was Achan destroyed, but also all that he possessed; property; animals; family; silver; gold; everything that he had was stone to death and then burned to make sure that they all died. How is it, that we as Children of God say we are Serving God, and have not yet fully Surrendered to God; there seems to be a lot of baggages that we are carrying with our salvation, a lot of other gods; when the only thing we should be carrying is the Cross that God called us to carry; the Responsibility to share with others concerning The Light of The World.

Let The Church Be The Church; and let the World Be the World. The job of The Church is to produce Believers of Jesus Christ Daily; that The Light of God Will Shine Brighter and brighter for this present Generation and for the Generation to come. The job that the World seeks to accomplish, is to stop The Church from becoming The Light of God. Therefore, The Ingredience of the World has no place in The Church. Can a man put new wine into an old bottle; can we put new clothes to an old raiment? NO, NO, NO; cannot work; will never work. For those of us who are of the belief that there is nothing wrong with the Decorations; look at this for a minute: Is it that I'm the only one up to now, have identified that there is something wrong with the Decorations; I think not! Or is it that others have seen the seed growing long before, but was just afraid to say anything about it, or else it may result in the number of the people coming to Church being less than what is desired; it will result in not having the support of someone in The Church that has influence of money? Judge for yourself, are we not hypocrites! Is the World, even as we speak, is it not a Big Influence in The Church; a Big Distraction? _____.

If we have clearly identified that The Church has reached a level that it is willing to bend down, and to acclimatize ourselves to the World, because of the gods we refuse to let go; then, is the World not influencing The Church! What's next? Are we going to create our own Doctrine, as to why certain customs and gods must be a part of our lives, thus allowing these Customs to be a part of The Church of The Living God. Search The Scriptures for in them we think we have Eternal Life; is there anywhere in The Bible, that, that which resembles The Living God, ever mixed with the other gods?

There is found in The Book of first Samuel Chapter 5. The Philistines took The Ark of The Covenant of God, and placed it in their own temple before their own gods; the story reveals that the Philistines god which is known as Dagon was a statue that was uprightly placed to stand before The Ark of GOD; it also revealed that they came to view Dagon their god on the second day of trying to mix their gods with The True Power Of The Almighty GOD; it was then they discovered that their god Dagon was fallen down from an upright stance, to now being upon his face to the ground before The Ark Of GOD; and the head of Dagon being cut off, along with the palms of his hands, leaving only the stump.

Before this happened, they came on the first day and realized that Dagon was fallen on his face towards The Ark of God; by this action they never took heed. They were also plagued greatly for having The Ark of The Living God. The Bible also Reveals that when King David sought to transfer The Ark of God to Jerusalem; there was a man named Uzzah, that put forth his hands to catch The Ark of The Living

God from falling; by this foolish action, The Anger of The Lord Was Kindled against Uzzah, and God Smote him for his errors. 2 Samuel Chapter 6.

It is also seen in The Book of Daniel Chapter 5. King Belshazzar took of the Vessels of The Lord's House and drank in it, he and his friends. Has we read we will realize that this was very destructive for King Belshazzar. I hope we have realized the Point; God Cannot MIX; therefore, It is time for us to Choose The God Who Is GOD. How is it that we are going to obtain GOD Which Is Light, and still hold unto darkness / other gods.

Have we ever tried turning on a light in a dark room? What happens? Yes, that's correct; the darkness is completely gone. Therefore, We can actually measure ourselves, to see exactly how much Light is truly in our Salvation. If we don't realize that there is a problem now; how is it that our children which is the Generation to come, going to accept change to know that this is not The Standard of God. The children of tomorrow will say, this is what I've been trained to do, therefore that's what they will follow. And if The Church continues to be Diluted; then, are we ever going to become The Lamb's Bride, The Wife of Christ? Let's examine me, am I ever going to become The Lamb's Bride, considering the custom that is now. No wonder The Bible Said:

"Let every man work out his own Salvation with fear and trembling; redeeming the times because the days are evil".

The Lord Gave me Instructions to mention the story of a young man in The Bible; the young man goes by the Name of Gideon; the story can be found in The Book of Judges 6-8. Gideon a Man of God, spoken to be a mighty man of valour. He was such a person because he lived in a time when, what we call trouble in Church because of the World's influence, would look like paradise to The Children of Israel. In that time when Idolatry was the name of the day and season; the Children of Israel openly served Baal. This man Gideon was called by God to work for Him; once he knew that God Was Certainly on his side, he boldly went and cast down the Altar of Baal and cut down the Grove.

The Lord Is Asking the Question to those of us in our Churches:

- CAN I DEPEND ON YOU TO BE A GIDEON.
- CAN I DEPEND ON YOU TO BE A MIGHTY MAN OF VALOUR. My House need Fixing.
- My People need to be told of what My Will and Commands are. My People need to Learn about Holiness.
- My People need to be prepared for The Coming of The Lord.
- Are you available to be My Chosen Vessel?
- Are you My Gideon?
- _____.

God Needed Gideon to Stand up for Him; because the only way The Children of Israel could get Deliverance was only if they stopped from worshipping IDOLS / strange gods. We wonder why God's Children are not getting the deliverance they should be receiving from GOD; it is clear as water; there is too much Idol worshipper in God's House; therefore, God Cannot Deliver, because GOD Cannot Mix with Darkness because He Is Light. I remember when The Lord Sent me to Perform a work for Him; He Gave me the Message that Says:

"A CALL FOR HOLINESS; GET BACK TO HOLINESS".

It's been almost two years, and this Message has become a theme song in The House of God, for all to understand, what The Values of The Church Are. Talking about the influence of the World; let's look on this for a moment: If the World is influencing The Church, of which it is; then what would be the best way to disguise that influence? Some of the methods that the World uses to let us believe that we are ok, is to Teach the younger Generation by means of Television; Radio; Tablets; MP3 players; Computers; and Telephones etc. To say that everyone is doing wrongs, and they are ok; therefore, You can do it too. We look on the Television and people are living all manner of Ungodly lifestyle; which trains our children to become living idolaters, pleasing themselves and the devil; therefore, Separating us from The Favors of The Almighty God.

The World is working overtime to gather as many souls they can influence, and it is sad to say, that the World is also gathering souls in The Church. What is The Church Doing? Is The Church going to continually say that God Will Fix The Church; has The Church not yet realized that while we wait on something that God Has Given us The Power to do for ourselves; that the youths are being Enticed by the Serpent, and is being lead far away from God; that when we have awoken out of our Slumber, if we ever will awake; there is nothing we can no longer do to keep the youths Interested in GOD.

Awake, awake, awake GOD's Gideon; God Is Calling you to do a Job, that only you can do. Don't allow the words to catch us which says: IF I HAD KNOWN. There is one thing that we can ask ourselves to justify our decisions, this is it:

- Did God Told you that it is ok for you to wear your decorations being A Child of God?
- Did he Tell you to wear anything you would want to wear?
- Did God Tell you, that as long as you have money, you can buy your way into Heaven?
- Did God Say to you that Holiness is not important; judge for yourself?

The Bible Says in Romans 12:1.

"I Beseech you therefore, brethren, by The Mercies of God, that ye present your bodies a living sacrifice, Holy, Acceptable unto God, which is your reasonable service".

I remember being a Young People's Director, I tried my very best to do what God Would Have me to do; I remember the time came, that The Church I attended first, thought that I was being too strict, therefore, They needed to vote me out of the position. I remember having an experience that Jesus Christ went through. On the day of the vote, The Church was filled with members that wasn't even a part of The Young People's Ministry, The Church was filled with people that wasn't coming to Church, The Church was full, having a minority of True Christians, and having a majority of backsliders and part time

Christians. Who was set in their will, to make sure that their votes went against me. In all the vote there was only one person who got up, and said that they were not in support of the decision of the vote. My question to you is this; do you want to be a part of a Church, that their influence comes from how they feel about you, or do you want to be a part of a Church, that all decisions are completely Influence by The Almighty God.

Remember the job God Called us to accomplish; not to be rich, but be The CHURCH, enriched with His Words; not to be popular, but to be The LIGHT OF THE WORLD; not to be common, but to be TRULY SPECIAL, Royal Priesthood, Holy Nation, Peculiar People; not to be doing what everyone else is doing, but to be doing and becoming what GOD NEED US TO BECOME; not to be ordinary, but to become SON'S OF GOD.

There is one thing that I've gotten to realize; If we don't know that we are DIFFERENT, then we will not behave like we are different; one of my Instructor in school taught me that, when a man have truly learnt; then that man's ATTITUDE must also learn. There is a saying that goes like this:

"You can't throw powder on black bird, because he will shake it off".

This was mainly spoken of by The Man of God Bishop Austin Whitfield. Yes, we were very black before we came to The Lord; now that we say we are Converted, are we still Black! Are we still Sinners! Have we discovered THE BLOOD that washed away all sin to make us CLEAN?

Now this is what The Lord Is Asking of us to Do, if it is that we have been Changed; Washed by The Blood and Redeemed. God Is Asking us to Create an Atmosphere in our own lives that will Affect The Church, that others will come and desire to be saved just like we are Saved; Create an Atmosphere that people will not see you the individual, but will see Christ Jesus in you, which brings forth The Light. Create an Environment that other Saint can actually picture the Future of their Children growing up in; an Environment that is strongly influenced and lead by The Hands of The Almighty God.

Israel had a Strong Relationship with God, because there was the evidence to prove to all people that The Almighty God Is Their Very Present Help In All Situations. Let us accept the challenge to Create an Environment for the Generation coming, to desire not what the World is manufacturing but to receive of all that God Has to Offer us. If we do not take heed to the warning, to STOP ALLOWING THE WORLD TO INFLUENCE THE CHURCH; then those of us who are living now would have already failed not only God, but have failed the Generation which is to come, because we got the warning to STAND; and instead of standing, we sat down and allowed what is happening now, to continue to happen.

Bad spirits and bad influence spread faster than Good Behavior; if we turn a blind eye on all the bad things; bad influence in The Church, when it is, that we are in the Position to do something about it, to stop the breathing of this spirit, then it is sad to say that we are going to live with the consequences of our errors. Our children didn't failed; we Failed. If this Generation is determined to succeed, then the Generation to come will be in a much better position to reach to a higher level in God, to welcome The Coming of The Lord if He Delays His Coming for the next Generation.

One of the main lesson we should learn from this Message is; if we don't MORTIFY the World from our own lives and family, then the World cannot be mortified from The Church. It starts with one, before it can expand or grow; one man can make a difference; will you be that one man. If we are not serious about GOD, then GOD Will Never Be Serious about us. Remember these Words from The Lord:

"With the merciful thou wilt show thyself merciful; with an upright man thou wilt show thyself upright; with the pure thou wilt show thyself pure; and with the forward thou wilt show thyself forward". Psalms 18:25&26.

A Froward person is someone who is willfully Contrary; which means that they know that something is wrong and presumptuously do what is wrong. To this person, God Says that His Appearance to him will be of that man's own discipline; it would be like looking into a mirror. Whatsoever we sow, that will we reap.

I Hope that this Message Has Inspired A Believer of God, I know it has Inspired me; let us seek to keep on improving ourselves in The Lord. May The Lord Continue to Bless you, and Prosper you. All Glory Be unto The Matchless Name of Jesus Christ, Our Soon Coming King. From the Servant of The Lord; Pastor Lerone Dinnall.

STOP ALLOWING THE WORLD TO INFLUENCE OUR PERSONAL LIVES, THEN IT WILL BE SEEN THAT THE WORLD CANNOT INFLUENCE THE CHURCH!

Awaken From Sleep!

Message # 48   Date Started January 17, 2017.
                                 Date Finalized January 29, 2017.

Isaiah 40:3-8.

"The voice of him that crieth in the wilderness, prepare ye the way of The Lord, make straight in the desert a highway for our God. Every valley shall be exalted, and every mountain and hill shall be made low: and the crooked shall be made straight, and the rough places plain: and The Glory of The Lord Shall Be Revealed, and all flesh shall see it together: for The Mouth of The Lord Hath Spoken It. The voice said, cry. And he said, what shall I cry? All flesh is grass, and all the goodliness thereof is as the flower of the field: the grass withereth, the flower fadeth: because The Spirit of The Lord Bloweth Upon It: surely the people is grass. The grass withereth, the flower fadeth: but The Word of our God Shall Stand For ever".

I Greet All My Father's Children in The Wonderful Matchless Name of Jesus Christ, The Risen Saviour. It is Truly an Honour to present another Inspiring Message, Manufactured by The Spirit of our God. Awaken from Sleep, what does that mean, and what is the interpretation of this Message that God Has Given? There is a True understanding that exist, and this is a fact; many people and even those of us who are Christians, are not even sure of what it takes, or what the feeling is like to Be Awaken. Because the truth is, we wake up each morning, accepting the World's Doctrine of what they declare

104

life to be, and for those of us who are Children of God, there is this false hope and teaching that appears within the place of Worship, that seeks only to make The Doctrine of Christ into a Message that will make everyone feel good about themselves even if they are in Sin. And then while Sleeping Spiritually, and living Physically, The Spiritual Will and Calling of God Past Us By The Way; because The Church is now of the Mind frame that to Be Spiritually Awaken is to ensure that we are present at Church every Sunday; not knowing that, that action only brings forth a marking of a Register. To be Spiritual Awaken, is it to have a Fellowship Card that reflect The Assemble or a specific Church that we attend?

Brother James wrote in The Book of James Chapter 2:14-26. In verse 18 he said:

"Shew me thy faith without thy works, and I will shew thee my faith by my works".

I made mention of this Scripture to clearly identify that the Physical Attributes / Show, must be Embedded with The Spiritual Anointing. James 2:26 Says:

"For as the Body without the spirit is dead, so faith without works is dead also".

Bishop Austin Whitfield would often speak to The Church by saying and I Quote:

"The Greatest thing in a man's life is to know, because a man who does not know, is a fool to what he don't know".

Let us ask ourselves this simple Question:

"I have been Serving God for _____ years, for those years can I truly say that I am walking in The Spirit of God, being Spiritual Awaken to God's Every Command"? _____.

Let me repeat the word Spirit of God, because we have not yet understand that if it is not The Spirit of God, there will be no Anointing, meaning no Spiritual Movement towards The Will and Purpose of God. We wonder why many things fail in Church, seeing that all the Disciplines of which man has set up are being followed and observed, but yet there is still no Victory! The answer to that statement is because there is no Leading of The Holy Ghost.

How is it that we are so sure that God Is Leading our Lives, and every Decisions that we are asked to make and to choose, those decisions are in agreement with what the Physical Man needs, which can never Please God.

Fact: Every Movement of The Anointing of God / Spirit of God, Will Provide a sense of Sacrifice to the person to whom The Spirit of God Is Moving In; because The Spirit of God Moves only to Please God, that God's Perfect Desires Will Be Manifested. When The Spirit of God Moves, the person in which God's Spirit Is Moving, will experience the sense of Sacrifice Being Burnt, and can only come into Agreement with God's Movement, and watch the results of what is being done; and many times what is being done, the Physical part of that person have no idea of why, when and for what reason it was done; but it is God that Declares that He Knoweth the End of Time from the very beginning of Time; and it is God that Moves His Spirit to Bring forth the Manifestation of His Perfect Glory. Jesus Christ Spoke to the woman at Jacob's Well in The Book of St John 4:21-24. Which Says:

"Jesus Saith unto her, woman, Believe Me, the hour cometh, when ye shall neither in this mountain, nor yet at Jerusalem, Worship The Father. Ye worship ye know not what: we know what we Worship: for salvation is of the Jews. But the hour cometh, and now is, when The True Worshippers Shall Worship The Father in Spirit and in Truth: for The Father Seeketh such to Worship Him. God Is A Spirit: and they that Worship Him must Worship Him In Spirit and In Truth".

Have a look at these words:

"Ye worship ye know not what".

Do we know Who and Why we are Worshipping?

The other thing to ask ourselves Is: Are we Worshipping God In Spirit and In Truth?

This Scripture allow us to Understand that without Spirit; "Hold on", this meaning The Spirit of God, that Brings forth the Manifestation of The True Anointing of God, and also Truth; without these two (2) Characteristics of God, there is no way a Person / Christian will reach The Qualified State of being A Worshipper for God.

Can I tell you the Truth; there are many Saints that are going to Church, that have not yet Identified that God Is The Center of their Worship. Many of our time goes towards activities that instead of Pleasing God, it brings forth Pleasure to the Pastor, Ministers, Missionaries, Bishops, Deacons, Brothers and Sisters or even ourselves; and this God Smells and Refuse to Grand Favors upon that which we Offer before Him. God Is Saying:

"Should I Accept this Offering, that only seeks to Promote Man, and thus Please the Desires of Flesh and not The Will and Glory of The Kingdom of God"?

There is something I must share with My Readers; I went to Kingston the other day, and went into a Restaurant to purchase a Lunch; while at the cashier to purchase my Lunch, there came a well Dressed Woman with her hand bag, spike heels, hair put together, asking for some assistance to open a container; upon looking on the Woman with my naked eye, I would have judged that this is a Woman that is taking good care of herself; it was not until the Woman came to the cashier where I was, that I realized and identified that not everything that looks good actually smells good. The smell of the Woman was so over bearing that I had to move very quickly away from the position I was, to now stand far off; then I discovered what God Must Be Experiencing, when it is that we come to Church and forget about the Sanctification in order for The Sacrifice to Be Accepted. Sanctification is in no way the Physical man, but it has everything to do with The Spiritual Man.

There is a saying that goes like this: Cleanliness is next to Godliness; note it never said that Cleanliness is Godliness; but it gives us an idea of what it takes to actually measure up to the Requirements of becoming Godly. Then we wonder why it is that we come to Church, and there is still no Spiritual Blessings; God's Favors upon our lives, but things remain the Same, which should not be. Every time an Accepted Offering Was Given to God in The Bible, something Supernatural Happen; so should it be with us, but what causes the decline of this action, it's because there is a lot of Blind people in Church, therefore blind is leading blind, therefore both will fall into the Ditch. There is indeed a great need for Spiritual Awakening; without Spiritual Awakening we are Stuck, just like The Children of Israel going around in Circles and not realizing that they are only fulfilling one Cycle of life which is the Physical Life.

There is a Sunday School I was privileged to be in; done by Overseer Lamar Banton; and he was Teaching on A Topic that I don't quite remember, but in that Message he made reference to the Fact that a lot of God's People are just like The Children of Israel, going around in Circles and not knowing that their life is but just A Big Circle. He said, and I Quote:

"Every year we end up doing the same thing, we get older but the conditions of life and our Attitude remains the same, and because year after year things around us are actually moving or growing, it therefore confuses us to make us think or believe that our life is actually Growing, which it is not; the trees around us grow, the people around us grow, business around us grow, but we are not realizing that instead of growing up, we are moving in Circles".

And I learnt something from that Sunday School Teaching. If we are Children of God, there must be Growth or else we will find ourselves being good for nothing else but just to be cut down and thrown in the fire to be burned; and be labelled as a Un Productive Fruit or Vineyard.

There is something of Great Importance that I would have My Readers to Understand, coming from the explanations that is written in the Webster's Dictionary. Now according to the Dictionary the word Awaken derives from the word Awake which is indeed a VERB, therefore, being identified as an Action; and it States:

"To Rouse from sleep, to make active or alert; rouse: To emerge from sleep".

Now this is the meaning I like the most, which basically explains the Mind Frame of what God Is Asking from His People.

"To Become Active or Alert; To Become CONSCIOUS of something: Finally Awoke to the Facts".

Have you ever been in Church and realize certain Movements, and in these Movements, there seems to be no one that is Alert or

Conscious of the Devices of the Enemy, but it seems to be a spirit that have overtaken every member, and there is no one to stand up and say this is not The Will of God; this is not what God Require from His People or His Church. And to move away from The Church Circle, because many of us seems to believe that the only place for Spiritual Awakening is in Church; what about when we are at Work, and The Lord Is Revealing His Anointing over our lives pertaining to what He Would Have Us To Manifest, and I'm not necessarily talking about seeking to Erect change in an Institution that man have establish, but rather trying to point out that we are so asleep Spiritually that when things are happening around our Circle, we just don't seem to be able to see that Prayer is needed at that time to War off the spiritual attacks that are heading our direction.

What about when we are at Home; Is there not the need for us to Be Spiritually Alert? The hard conclusion to accept, is the fact that many Saints will not be Awaken, reason being, to be Spiritual Awaken simple means that a person have come to the conclusion that something is ultimately wrong in their lives, and is desirous to seek a change for what is wrong in their lives, thus understanding that the only medium through which we can reach to a place of Spiritual Awakening, is to First admit that we are on the wrong path way; and whatever causes us to be on the wrong path, must have come through the evidence of SIN; and this is what most of us will never Admit to; because for some strange reason The Children of God have found themselves in a Position that we just don't like to accept the fact that we have sinned, and that sin will always be present as long as we live in this flesh; to allow us to now be in a Position that we can Ask God Continually to Cleanse us from the Sins we have committed. Unless we has Christians come to the realization that sin needs to be washed away, then there can be no Spiritual Awakening, and that's a Fact.

Sin is to be compared to Heavy Loads that stops A Child of God from Manifesting What God Requires for us to Manifest; therefore as often as it takes to Confess our Sins, and to be in Fasting to be Cleanse from the Heavy loads, this will be of great benefit to us as Children of God. I taught the Members of My Assembly, to make sure that in their walk with God, that they must always remember that there is a need for The Prayer of Confession of Sins; because The Bible Says in 1 John 1:8-10.

"If we say that we have no sin, we deceive ourselves, and the truth is not in us. If we confess our sins, He Is Faithful and Just to Forgive us our sins, and to Cleanse us from all unrighteousness. If we say that we have not sinned, we make Him a liar, and His Word Is Not In Us".

How can we seek for Cleansing or Spiritual Awakening without first acknowledging that there is Dirt and Spots that needs to be washed away?

There is A Story in The Bible that Taught me as a Pastor a great deal about being Sanctify Before The Sacrifice Can Be Accepted. And that's The Story in The Book of Judges Chapter 19 through to Chapter 21. In summary, there was this Levite that had a concubine, after departing the home of the concubine's father, he and his company decided to spend the night in one of the towns that were of The Tribe of Israel, being The Tribe of Benjamin; the Benjamites treated this man and his company very bad, In that they took the man's concubine and abused her for the duration of a whole night leading to the break of day; by this action The Levite could not believe that he was treated in a manner such as this, from one of The Tribes which was of his own family lineage. The Levite had the option to retire in the land of the Jebusites, but being an Israelites he rather to take a longer journey to ensure that he was amongst brethren or so he taught!

After the Benjamites mistreated and abused this man's concubine, she came back to the Levite being battered, abused, and lifeless; the Levite took a knife and divided her body into twelve pieces and send it to all the coast of Israel.

Now when Israel gathered themselves to find out from the Levite what was the reason for this, and the Levite began to tell them what befall him from one of the Tribes of Israel; they all agreed that this was the heights of wickedness and thus send to the Tribe of Benjamin for these wicked men to be brought to justice; this however was refused by the Benjamites. This action resulted in Israel desiring to war with the Benjamites, of which they went to The House of God to ask Request of God to fight; and The Lord Responded by Telling them to let the Tribe of Judah go up first. The Tribe of Judah went up, and they were defeated, twentytwo thousand men (22,000).

The Israelites encouraged themselves; they went and wept before God until evening, and ask The Lord again if they should go up and fight with the Benjamites; The Lord Told them to Go Up the second time, and the results were the same, they were defeated again; this time eighteen thousand (18,000) men died. It was not until The Children of Israel realized that God Was A God of Order, that Required of them to do what was necessary for them to do, in order for them to receive The Favors from God, to be able to be victorious in the Battle.

The Bible Said that The Israelites came to God the Third time, with weeping, and sat before The Lord with Fasting until evening, they offered Burnt Offerings and Peace Offerings before The Lord; then asked The Lord if they should go up; of which The Lord Told them to Go Up, and this time because The Children of Israel finally realized or have been Spiritually Awaken to the fact that for God to Judge, to Bring forth Victory and Favors, there must be first a Cleansing / Sanctification before the Acceptance of a Sacrifice can be Granted; and furthermore The Lord Told Israel to make the Tribe of Judah to go up first, because if God Is Going to Judge sin; should not The Tribe which is said to be The Law Giver, which knew God's Law, should not they be the first to be Judged? Because in God's Eye, He Considers judgment to be Complete and not partly done as how a Natural man would have demonstrated Judgment.

God Looked on Israel as being One Nation, and not Twelve Tribes. Judah was Judged and Destroyed because they were the ones that knew God's Law; therefore, They should have been The First Tribe to bring Israel into Worship for the Cleansing of Sins, to allow God to Bring forth Victory.

To whom much is Given, will much also be Required from God. God Cannot and Will Not Bring forth Victory while there is still the evidence of Sin and lack of Understanding of God's People to know what to do. Isaiah 59:1&2. This story should make us all search ourselves very careful before we go to God with any Request. Remember these words Sanctify Before The Sacrifice.

There is no Spiritual Awakening if we still believe and are determined that there is no Sin. We will continue to go before God with our Request; and God Will Continue To Say Yes, I Will Do It For You; not realizing that, that answer comes with Conditions Applied. In God's Eye our Request is Granted Providing that we will do what is Expected for us to do; and many times, what is expected for us to do takes some time; it may take days, months or years, it may cause many people to be sick or even die, as we have seen in The Book of Judges, but it all depends on the time that we have realized that there must be a Sanctification of our own lives before God, in order for the Sacrifice with our request to be finally Granted.

God Work Speedy when it is that His People are of The Knowledge of what is Required of them to do from God. Again, God Works Slow, when it is that His People have a blockage of Spiritual Understanding that will take some time for His People to know what is Required by God; therefore, Many of our Request take Years to come to Fulfillment. And again God Will Not Come Through, when it is that His People will not fulfill what God Requires us to Do.

We must always remember that Relationship with God is like looking at ourselves in a mirror; whatever we Present to God of our Sacrifice, it is the same that is to be Delivered to us from The Favors of God; and again that which is our Relationship with God, can be seen in the company that we are around. We can actually see a Manifestation of ourselves in the persons that we associate with.

There must be the Understanding Already Fixed in the lives of God's People to know that God Can Do All that He Say He Can Do; but there is always Conditions Applied. Before God's Eyes, He Sees every person and already knows every Request; God Knows the path on which each Saints will travel, therefore, There is no surprise that anyone can spring forth that God Will Be Shocked. God Knew that Adam and Eve would have Sinned, and there was nothing God Would Have Done to Alter that Event, because God's Main Mission is that of Kingdom Building; and God's Kingdom could not have been

Built then, because there was the evidence of the spirit of Envy that consumed Lucifer, and also consumed Adam and Eve.

And in God's Kingdom Building, every Saint that is Destined for The Kingdom, are those who have Mastered Free Will; meaning, these Saints have Mastered Life's Cross Road Puzzle, to always be in a Position to Choose the right pathway even though that pathway may be Rough, Painful, Hard to Sow Seed on, this pathway may not accommodate the company of friends and family members, the right pathway may be a Lonely journey; the pathway to Righteousness is very narrow and can only accommodate a few people at any one time, because the path to Righteousness can be compared to a Bottle's Neck, or that of a Strainer, because there is so much Restriction, the journey is often times very slow and difficult to walk on; it will even become Frustrating, and this is where Spiritual Awakening Shines Her Light, to allow us to See what God Would Have Us To See, to Understand that our Lives is not being Delayed, but instead it's being Spiritually Set Up for Great and Prosperous things in God's Will.

Frustration chips in when we take our Focus from that which matters, and start to have a look on what the World is achieving and how fast the World is Accomplishing what they are Accomplishing.

We must remember the words of Asaph in The Book of Psalms 73.

"Truly God is good to Israel, even to such as are of a clean heart. But as for me, my feet were almost gone; my steps had well nigh slipped. For I was envious at the foolish, when I saw the prosperity of the wicked. For there is no bands in their deaths: but their strength is firm. They are not in trouble as other men; neither are they plagued like other men. Therefore pride compasseth them about as a chain; violence covereth them as a garment. Their eyes stand out with fatness: they have more than heart could wish. They are corrupt, and speak wickedly concerning oppression: they speak loftily. They set their mouth against the heavens, and their tongue walketh through the earth. Therefore his people return hither: and waters of a full cup are wrung out of them. And they say, how doth God knows? And is there knowledge in The Most High? Behold, these are the ungodly, who prosper in the world; they increase in riches. Verily I have cleansed my heart in

113

vain, and washed my hands in innocency. For all the day long have I been plagued, and chastened every morning. If I say, I will speak thus; behold, I should offend against the generation of thy Children". Verse 16&17 says: "When I thought to know this, it was too painful for me; until I went into the sanctuary of God; then understood I their end".

Until Asaph was Spiritually Awaken, then he understood that these Men were not on The Foundation of God's Word; therefore, They could not stand when The Test of life has begun. The right pathway may even lead to our Deaths to be Martyr for Christ. It is for us to Choose the right path to walk on, comes what may to Inherit Eternal Life.

However, God Had Already Put in Adam and Eve the main Ingredient of His Likeness to be able to Choose the Right Path; this they refused to choose because of the spirit of Envy that consumed their Mind and Heart. Even this event did not Shocked God, because God Would Have Already Put Plans in Place for Man's Redemption from Sin, through The Sacrifice of Jesus Christ.

We wonder many a times why it is that things happen to us Suddenly; unfortunate things, which it seems we have no control of these things happening to us. There is a sad Fact; and this is to know that we have the Capability only through The Spirit of God if we are Awaken, to actually be in Touch with The Spiritual Side of Things, before the Physical part of life begins to Form. Because many of us is not Awaken, we lose out from knowing what is in The Mind Of The Unknown; this Unknown Is God.

Deuteronomy 29:29 Says:

"The Secret things belong unto The Lord our God: but those things which are revealed belong unto us and to our children for ever, that we may do all the words of this law".

This may seem Meaningless to many, but for God's People that are seeking to Climb the Ladder of Spirituality, we know that this is True. For example, The Lord Jesus Christ Said that we shall be able to do the Works that He Had Done, and also Greater Works than these which He Had Done, shall we that are following in His Footsteps be able to Do. St John 14:12. And while there is still the Speech that we Declare that we are Serving God, but still there is no Evidence of the

Greater Work, and it is even now, we are Satisfied with just being called A Christian without the Evidence of the Greater Works! And the only reason we find ourselves in the Position of being so called Satisfied; is because even now we are Spiritually Sleeping, and need to be Awaken from the Slump that we are in.

Jesus Told His Disciples in The Book of St Matthew Chapter 24:42-44. Which Says:

"Watch therefore: for ye know not what hour your Lord doth come. But know this, that if the goodman of the house had known in what watch the thief would come, he would have watched, and would not have suffered his house to be broken up. Therefore be ye also ready: for in such an hour as ye think not The Son of man cometh".

St Mark Chapter 13:35-37 Says:

"Watch ye therefore: for ye know not when the Master of the house cometh, at even, or at midnight, or at the cockcrowing, or in the morning: lest coming suddenly He find you **SLEEPING**. And what I say unto you I say unto all, Watch".

The word sleeping there is not referring to the sleep we take when we are tired and desire rest; but instead the Sleeping The Lord Is Warning us about, is that of Spiritual Blindness, we are not able to See and to Understand that which God Need us to See and to Understand; therefore, Although we have been Baptized and going to Church often; that does not necessarily means that we are Spiritually Awaken.

There are sometimes, to be Spiritual Awaken means, we just have to be alone at times, to Hear and to Understand the Commands of what God Would Have Us To See in order for us to walk in a path that will ensure that we are untouched by the Enemy; and many times, that which God Asked for us to Accomplish will not be what the Crowd or Majority of The Church Assembly is doing. Spiritual Awakening is at times a LONELY ROAD; but it is a NECESSARY ROAD, to enable us to enter through The Gates of Heaven.

To Give My Readers an example of how Lonely the road can get, I will share one of my Testimony. I was in Church one day, The Church I previously attended, and I was observing the Worship, and the Movements of what was happening in The House of God, and right there when it is that Members should have known what it is that they should be doing to Attract God in a Positive way; Members was instead doing the opposite of what it takes to Please God, and this wasn't the first time it happened; and even though I tried to bring some type of order to what was going on, my attempts were Futile.

It was there and then I saw A Vision, and I won't say what was the Vision, but I saw something, and I saw what God Was Going To Do; but when I tried to understand what I saw and the meaning of what I saw, I went and tried asking other members if they saw anything without declaring what I saw, and I could not find any that saw what I saw, of whom I asked. I went home and Prayed to God to Explain what I saw because it troubled my soul; The Lord Responded by Telling me to call a particular Minister and asked him what he saw, without telling him what I saw; that I did, and The Minister was able to tell me what he saw with the only difference being, I saw a Sword, and he saw a Big Fire Ball, doing the same purpose of what we both saw. I shared this Testimony to let us understand that being Difference doesn't mean that you're Weird; we all move according to The Manifestation of The Spirit of God in us, especially when we are Walking in The Spirit.

The Lord Revealed that Spiritual Awakening is to Fully Understand the Senses of the Physical Man and also know that it has it place; then to Come into or to Elevate or to Awake to The Senses of The Almighty GOD; this is an experience that has to be Born in us. When we are Spiritually Awaken, we will Move the way God would have for us to Move, we would Automatically See What God Needs For Us To See, to the Measurement to which God Permits for us to See; we would Feel things, that no one else is able to feel because of The Spirit of God that Lives in us; we are now able to Smell danger from a far.

Have you ever been in a position that The Holy Ghost is just keeping you away from something or someone? What do you think The Spirit of God Is Doing? That's it; it is trying to Alert Us to know that there is Danger Ahead, of which we may not yet have the level of Anointing to Overcome the Elements of the Atmosphere that is Ahead.

The Spirit of God Enhances our Spiritual Abilities that we can also Taste The Sacrifice of Our Worship or of the Assembly of God, to show Difference to us, to allow us to Understand what is Accepted from God, from that which is Rejected by God; yes we can Taste it! The Spirit of God Manifest Its Movements in us by the Three Main Principles / Gifts or Spirit of The God Head, by that of: Understanding; Knowledge and Wisdom.

By these A Child of God that is Spiritually Awaken will be Able according to The Measurement of God Which God Allows; they will be able to Manage the Affairs of Personal life and also The Affairs of God, in keeping in God's Will. It doesn't matter what devices the enemy plans, The Mind of God in the life of A Child of God Will Be More Than Able To Counteract Every Plans and Traps that the enemy has Fixed.

The God Head Is The Power of The Alpha and Omega, which means that God Is The Living Alphabet of both Spiritual Life and Physical Life; therefore, If the enemy spells in A Child of God's life, a word that they will lose their Home, their Husband or Wife, their Children or anything at all, and even if it is Fixed; The Alpha and Omega which is The Fullness of The God Head will Find Suitable Words within Himself to Manifest again all that A Child of God has lost, and Reimburse a double portion. To Understand The God Head is of Great Importance for A Child of God; with this Revelation comes the Manifestation that every Child of God that is Spiritually Awaken, is actually Untouchable; Yes I said that word:

"UNTOUCHABLE".

What did God Said to Joshua; according to The Book of Joshua Chapter 1:5-9:

"There shall not any man be able to stand before thee all the days of thy life: as I Was With Moses, so I Will Be With Thee: I Will Not Fail Thee, nor Forsake Thee. Be strong and of a good courage: for unto this people shalt thou divide for an inheritance the land, which I Sware unto their fathers to Give them. Only be thou strong and very courageous, that thou mayest observe to do according to all the Law, which Moses My Servant commanded thee: turn not from it to the right hand or to the left, that thou mayest prosper whithersoever thou goest. This Book of the law shall not depart out of thy mouth; but thou shalt meditate therein day and night, that thou mayest observe to do according to all that is written therein; for then thou shalt make thy way prosperous, and then thou shalt have good success. Have not I Command thee? Be Strong and of a good courage; be not afraid, neither be thou dismayed: for The Lord Thy God Is With Thee whithersoever thou goest".

And this was said in a time when it was known that The Spirit of God Came Upon His People; how much Great an Effect is that Promise now that The Living Spirit of God Is Now In Us, Living with us and never departs as long as we live for God! Should we consider ourselves broken, when The God who we Serve Can Make us all over again and better than before? The Lord Jesus Christ Declare and also Decreed in The Book of St Matthew Chapter 28:18 by Saying:

"All Power is Given unto Me in Heaven and in Earth".

Now if All Power belongs to our Saviour, why are we worried; concerning about if we lose material things on this journey! Is our God not more than Capable to Speak and it will be Manifested again and better than before?

The Lord Revealed to me, that concerning The God Head, which is The Use of The Three Main Spirit of The God Head, which is Understanding, Knowledge and Wisdom; which goes by the Order in which it is set. Which means that A Child of God will First obtain the seed of Understanding, which then brings birth to The Gift / Fruit of Knowledge, which then Manifest Wisdom, and Wisdom shows how these Tools of The God Head should be Used. That when A Child of God has been Spiritually Awaken and is able to USE The God Head Effectively, there will now be realized by that Child of God, what is Sin from what is not Sin; because there are many things that a person that is Natural may Judge to be Sin; but in The Eyes of God, that which was done was the Use of The God Head to avoid a Greater damage or to kill the Birth of a Sin being committed.

Let me give an example of what The Lord Revealed: Have you ever been in a position that you were asked suddenly to commit to a task or an assignment, of which under the pressure of that commitment you immediately said yes without having thought out what you're getting involved with. And it is by Teaching and by Custom that whatever you have committed to, you would have to Fulfill. Now let's say that, that which you have committed to do, was in fact A Trap that is destined for the destruction of your Soul or to put chains on your feet, to restrict The Holy Anointing Movement of The Spirit of God in your Life. Would you now be Eager to fulfill that which you have already made a promise to do? Think very hard and long on the answer that you will give.

The Lord Revealed that because The Main Duty of His Spirit is to always be A Protector for our Soul from the Hands of the Enemy; The Lord Reveals that because it is that we at times are not as Awaken as we should be, these Traps and Snares seek to Creep upon us, for the main purpose of Entrapment. The Lord Reveals that it is no Sin if A Child of God Ignorantly makes a commitment of which they are not aware that it is A Trap; which then The Spirit of God which is The Revelation of everything Hidden, Reveals the Intentions of what is Set and Fixed to destroy A Child of God's Life.

In God's Eye we have not Sinned if we now choose, by The Direction of The Spirit of God, not to fulfill that which the Physical part of our life has committed to fulfill in Ignorance; because we must always remember that we are indeed Servants to God and His Will Being Done in our Lives; than to man and the requirements of Man's Customs and Rules. Because, what God Deems as Sin, is that which a person is well Knowledgeable of, and being Knowledgeable and having the Understanding of what will happen after such a Sin is Committed; that's what is Manifested as Sin in God's Eye. But in Man's eye, they now have something to Judge us by, to say yes, we have Sinned a Great Sin. Remember Peter, James and John, speaking to The High Priest, when they were commanded by Man's Custom not to Preach or Teach in The Name of The Lord Jesus Christ; what did they say? They Said:

"We ought to obey God rather than men". Acts 5:29.

Question; which is better, the Teaching of Men and his Customs, which is in fact something that has been Revealed to them; or The Teachings and The Revelations of The Almighty God, which from Him Comes also The Teachings of that which we learned from Man's Instructions and also that which has not yet been Revealed? Why do you think Adam and Eve got the Punishment of Death when they ate the Fruit and Disobeyed God's Command? Adam and Eve were not Ignorant of what they did, they were well knowledgeable of what God's Commandment were, and they willfully by Free Will choose to accept the spirit of Envy and Sinned against God.

Yes, it is a Fact, Adam and Eve Died the very moment they ate of the Fruit of Knowledge of Good and Evil. God Could No Longer Commune with Adam face to face, which means that Spiritual Life was now taken away from Adam. The Church needs to Understand that if were not able to see what God Need us to See, then it is a Fact that we are Spiritually Dead. Here is a Truth: there is a lot of DEAD PEOPLE going to Church. Believe that!

The Ingredience of Spiritual Awakening must be found in The Words of God and must also be Established by The Word and Works of God, through a key Ingredient called Patient; remember that one of the devils main tools is to cause God's People to do things in haste without us using The Spirit Man which is The Holy Ghost to Manifest what is The True Revelation of what is hidden as a Snare and Trap to cause us to fall.

Bishop Austin Whitfield would often say, and I Quote:

"Once we are in The Spirit, we cannot Sin".

Which should make us to realize that the only way we sin, is when our lives is in a State that we are Spiritually Asleep.

The Bible Said:

"Walk in The Spirit, that we will not fulfill the lust of the Flesh". Galatians 5:16-18.

Galatians 5:22-26. Speaks of the Fruits of the Spirit, we can all have a read to further understand Spiritual Awakening.

I Give All Honor and Glory to God that Formed Heaven and Earth, The God that Revealeth Secrets, that we are able to keep Alive until He Comes back for His Chosen People. From the Servant of God and The Ministry of The Church of Jesus Christ Fellowship Savannah Cross Ltd. I Remain your company in life; Pastor Lerone Dinnall.

Awaken From Sleep!

Stepping Out Of The Ways, To Now Being Able To Walk In The Way.

Message # 70.

Date Started May 13, 2017
Date Finalized May 20, 2017.

St John Chapter 10:14-16.

"I Am The Good Shepherd, and Know My Sheep, and am known of mine. As The Father Knoweth me, even so Know I The Father: and I Lay down My Life for the sheep. And other sheep I have, which are not of this fold: them also I must bring, and they shall hear My Voice; and there shall be one fold, and one shepherd".

I Honour, Magnify and Offer Praises continually to The Invisible God, which can only be Identified by The Christ Like Character of His People. Glad am I no stranger to The Fellowship of The Blood of Jesus Christ our Soon Coming King. Privileged am I to be in this position that I can be of service through the writing of Messages on paper for God's People to read, to therefore receive a Greater Understanding of our walk with Christ.

I am a strong believer that Faith has Levels, and Understanding has Levels, Knowledge has Levels, and Wisdom has Levels; it is also my belief that Relationship with God Grows and out grows from one Level to a continual higher Level, which means that there can never be too much about knowing about The God that we are Serving.

It is also my belief that every Church that is present on the face of the Earth as long as they are recognizing that there is A God, then it is my belief through The Revelation of The Holy Ghost, that such a Church has A Relationship and Revelation with God The Father; weather The Church is called The Church of Jesus Christ, or The Church of The Living God, or Baptist Church, or The Seven Days Adventist etc. It doesn't matter what the name is or Denomination, I am certain that on any given day, if a person should enter the Assembly of one of these Denomination / Churches, I'm 100% certain that The Message will not be speaking about how to serve the Devil or to be his followers, but instead The Message will be to identify some level of Understanding about who God Is and seeking to Teach The Character of God to those who will aspire to change, therefore bringing forth a society that believes that God Exist.

A Commendation of Respect should be given to all Churches, Pastors, Bishops, Elders, Ministers, Missionaries, Overseers, Deacons, Brothers and Sisters, that are seeking to Teach and to Preach The Character of God The Father. It is by The Revelation of God, that God Has Revealed that All Nations, Languages, and Tongues belongs to Him; and it is out of these His People that God Has Chosen who it is that will be His Sheep that will Hear His Voice.

The Lord by Revelation Revealed that there will always be 10% of the people which is His Tithes, that are Chosen and Predestined to be a part of His Kingdom. Can you just imagine, being in A Church with One Thousand Members (1000), if this calculation is correct, and the Tithes is then 10% of the Assembly, that means that only One Hundred (100) Saints that are Stamped with Holiness would have been Chosen.

Note: I never said that we should start to count the Assemblies and pick out 10% that we think is Holy. No one can just look on a person and estimate or predict that such a person is Chosen by God for His Kingdom, because only God Alone Knows what is the Destiny of each Individual, and furthermore each individuals Destiny is wrapped up in their own Free Will towards God's Word. A Child of God should always demonstrate the Confidence that God Has Poured upon them because of their walk of Holiness with The Living God; A Confidence that is felt through every speech we make, and every step we take.

One of the Beauty about Being Holy for God, is that we are ONLY for God, and we need not anyone to tell us that we are walking on The Holy Path, because we Know; a desire for Holiness is our everything and everyday event. The Tithes of The Lord is Revealed as being Holy unto The Lord; therefore this sign demonstrate to us that if The Lord is indeed coming back for The Tithes of The Saints, it should be in our Understanding that one of The Requirement is to be and to remain to be Holy, because everything that moves away from being Holy is spelt Unholy. Holiness is simple, once A Child of God has The Mind for Holiness then it can be achieved easily, the meaning of Holiness in Bible terms and in God's Eye is simply:

"SEPARATING OURSELVES FROM EVERYTHING UNCLEAN, THUS ALLOWING GOD TO ALWAYS HAVE AN AVAILABLE TEMPLE FOR GOD'S USE".

Now the Challenge it set, and the target for Heaven is no longer a doubt of what is the Requirement to Inherit The Kingdom God; again I will repeat that the Requirement to Inherit Heaven is Holiness or Becoming The Tithes of The Saints that God Will Accept. Now this is certain and True; the Big Question that should be on our Minds is what are we willing to do about God's Standard? Will God Give to us a Free pass to Inherit His Kingdom because we attended Church for (42) years without knowing about Holiness, this number of years is considered to be one (1) hour in God's Eye? Will God Look the other way and lower His Standards because we paid Tithes of Money and other service for The Church without Holiness?

"Lord I prophesied in Thy Name; Lord I cast out devils, I visited the sick, widows and fatherless, Lord I gave my body to be burned for this Gospel, Lord I gave all my substance to the poor, Lord I was Baptized in The Name of The Lord Jesus Christ and Received The Gift of The Holy Ghost".

Without Holiness The Lord Will Profess, I never knew you: depart from me, ye that work Iniquity. St Matthew Chapter 7:15-23.

Studying The Bible and also by The Teaching of The Holy Ghost Revealed that for A Child of God to truly know and to have a meaningful Relationship with God, that Child of God must know about Holiness; and not only know, but love everything that moves in a direction of Holiness, because Holiness is The Character and Manifestation of The Almighty God. If we do not know about Holiness then it is certain, we have no Relationship and Revelation with God. Our Relationship is rather with The Church and The Members of The Church; because God only Comes into Relationship with those who are trying their best to walk A Holy life; and with The Help of God, we will be able to achieve the walk of Holiness through God's Revelation.

1 Corinthians 13:11.

"When I was a child, I spake as a child, I understood as a child, I thought as a child: but when I became a man, I put away childish things".

God by Revelation have not left us dry in Understanding, meaning; the very life we now live is a complete reflection to Teach us daily about growth and the importance for A Child of God to Grow; because if it is found that A Child of God refuses to Grow, then it remains that such A Child of God will remain at a Level of just being A Child in The Spirit, that have not yet been Born to Spiritual Maturity. And one of the main disadvantages of being and remaining to be A Child in The Spirit, is that A Child is accustom to make mistakes over and over again, until that Child is now born of the Understanding that Growth and Elevation is a must, to cause the doors of Mistakes to be closed forever.

We all can agree that when we were still A Child in the physical, that the lesson to learn our A,B,C, was of great importance; because without A,B,C, we would not be able to put words together, therefore allowing us to be able to spell and then to be able to read; but now that we have learnt our A,B,C, are we still desirous to go back in that same class room to again learn that which we have learnt? I think the answer is No. So is it in The Spiritual, while it remains to be good that there are a lot of Churches that are constant to Teach and Preach about The Living God; the thought still remains logging in the back of our Minds:

"Am I being taught something New by The Revelations of God, or is it that I'm just being taught what I've already learnt about last year in Sunday School"?

Is there still a need for us to be constantly being taught about the A,B,C, of knowing about God; Yes, the reminder of the A,B,C, of knowing about God is Good, because they Act as being a reminder of The Ten Commandments in The Bible, but are we going to remain at being Good; is it not time for The People of God to step out of being Good, to now walk into The Anointing of being Great, and then after we have fulfilled being Great, to now being able to walk into The Anointing of being and becoming Excellent in the Training and School Room of The Almighty GOD!

Here is a thought: How can we The Children of God Conquer The Power of Sin, if it is at present that our Minds is limited in The Knowledge of God? A Little Knowledge means a Little Authority to perform The Works of God; Great and Excellent Knowledge means that there will be Manifested A Great and Excellent Authority of The Power of God in our lives.

This is not A Message to condemn any Church, but instead to seek to inspire all Churches that has The Revelation that there is A Living GOD, to continue on the pathway of Good, and while on this pathway, to seek to move away from just being Good, to now becoming Great, and then when we have become Great, this Movement will aspire The Church / The Body of Christ to elevate to become Excellent in every Movement, in every Speech, in every Teaching and Preaching, in every Work for The Living God.

Here is a Fact: The World has become Excellent in manipulating the Minds of the future Generation that should take up the Mantle of continuing The Worship for God; and if The Church remains in a Movement of only being Good; then what will the Future look like for the Generation that is to come. While The Churches seek to remain and to exist as being Good for the World; the World is becoming Excellent in destroying our future Generation.

Fact: The Placement of The Church is not to remain Good, but rather to be and to become The Light of the World, A City that is set upon a hill for all to see and acknowledge that The Standard of God Remains Firm. While The Churches seek to remain Good, the World has taken the Position and Authority that we should have and should be walking in, to spoil that Position, as it was in the beginning when the Serpent tricked Eve to eat of the forbidden Fruit, thus causing our Forefather to lose their Rightful Position in this World.

It should be The Spirit Filled Church of God, meaning Saints that are living for God, we should be making all Decisions to be past for Law; but rather it is the opposite; people that know nothing about God is putting in place Rules and Laws that are putting Chains around the Necks of those who are Serving The Living God. Look at how far The Church as Fallen; we have an Origin and Foundation of God, that in the beginning of Time God Said let there be Light, and Light came forth; God Spoke to Abraham and said: Is anything too hard for God to Do? The Lord Spake to Moses that great leader, and told him; I AM THAT I AM. And also proved that very speech to everyone who oppose The Children of Israel.

The Church is coming from A Foundation, that God was Speaking to Moses on top of the Mountain, and the Mountain Quake by reason of The Power of God; it was so effective that the people cried for Moses to speak to God only, because they Feared that if they remained in and around The Presence of God, that they would have Died. So far has The Foundation Fallen that Church is in Progress and Sinners are comfortable to be in the assembly of The Righteous, no Fear, no thought and Mindset to surrender their lives over to God, because The Church remain at being Good for the World. And because we are Good for the World, we Compromise with the World thus causing The Glory of God that should be in The Church to now be Chased away from the very Temple of God.

Fact: People don't fear Churches anymore, because The Presence of God is Limited in Churches; because the Sinners comes to Church to Surrender to God and sees that the Minister that is to entertain them to come to God, is that same Minister or Missionary or Whoever, is the same person that is doing the same wrong Activity or even worse than what they are doing. Then we ask the Question: Why is people no longer coming to Church to give their lives over to God?

Fact: There is a saying that goes like this:

"The Truth Hurts".

Here is a Truth, The Churches have Fallen from The Likeness and Glory of God; it is no more what The Lord Command, or what The Lord Require; The Church has become a Den of thieves; with Members and Leaders only Interest being that of Money, and not about Souls. Don't be angry with me, it is The Lord that Allowed me to write this Message, and I Respect only THE ALMIGHTY GOD.

Stepping out of the ways to now being able to walk in the Way; this Message is not a calling for members to leave their Assemblies, but rather to elevate their way of living, from that of Good, to become Great, and then to elevate to become Excellent; and if it is that the environment that your around does not allow A Child of God to Grow, then it is the Responsibility and Free Will of that Child of God to seek The Perfect Way, to seek The Good Ground, that brings forth Excellent Fruits.

When I was first Commissioned by God to Build an Altar, The Message from God was Clear, which Says:

"A CALL FOR HOLINESS, TELL MY PEOPLE TO GET BACK TO HOLINESS".

From that day forward, that Message as stuck in My Head.

For individuals that are seeking to walk in The Excellent way, I recommend that we always remember that our Soul is the most Valuable possession, if we lose our Soul, then we would have lost everything; therefore, let us do all that is in our power to ensure that our Soul finds Rest. A reminder of The Word of God Says:

"Who will rise up for me against the evildoers? Or who will stand up for me against the workers of iniquity?" Psalms 94:16.

Here is a Question: Are we that person that The Lord is Seeking for to Stand up for Him; that our Good service will become Great service and our Great service will become Perfect / Excellent service? It is God's Requirement for Perfection.

St Matthew 5:48.

"Be ye therefore perfect, even as your Father which is in Heaven is perfect".

All Glory, Honour and Praise to The Mighty God, Jesus Christ The Lamb of God. From the Servant of God Pastor Lerone Dinnall and The Ministry of The Church of Jesus Christ Fellowship Savannah Cross Ltd.

Stepping Out Of The Ways, To Now Being Able To Walk In The Way.

Fear

Message # 8   Date Started September 23, 2016.
                               Date Finalized September 30, 2016.

All Glory and Praise to The King of kings and Lord of lords; The GOD who is ALPHA and OMEGA, The First and The Last; unto The GOD that LIVETH and was Dead, and behold Is ALIVE FOREVER MORE. Greetings to all My Fathers Children; I must say that I count all The Messages that God Has Given me to write as being Truly Special; but for this Topic that The LORD Has Inspired me to write by allowing me to see A Vision to Explain the meaning and the purpose of the word FEAR; I count this opportunity a great privilege, not only to write this Message that my fellow Brothers and Sisters in The Lord can know how to overcome the spirit of Fear, but also to be able to know for myself, that I can always be an Overcomer of Fear.

Let us establish some Facts: Fear is a spirit that if we continue to Feed or Entertain, will continue to Grow and Manifest; thus causing us to never be able to relinquish the very presence of what we feel by the Fear we possess. According to the Webster's Dictionary Which States:

"Fear is a distressing emotion aroused by impending danger, evil or pain; whether the threat is real or imagined. Fear is the feeling or condition of being afraid; being concern or anxiety".

The Dictionary also made mention of the Fear that a person has towards God; by expressing that it is a feeling of Reverential Awe.

While we can clearly say that The Fear of God is Good; because it keeps us away from doing that which is not pleasing in The Eyes of The Lord. On the other hand, the Fear of anything else can and will be destructive both to the spirit and body of any Individual.

I recently had a member of the assembly, discussing with me of her concerns pertaining to The Commands of The Lord. She told me that she was afraid to do wrong things, because it seems as if God's Eyes were constantly upon her. I told her that this was a Good Fear, because if there is a Spirit of Fear upon our life that prevents us from sinning, then that Presence from God should always be welcomed; which will result in us walking on Chalk line, not leaving ourselves to be exposed to danger.

The spirit of Fear that a person Develops, and I say Develop because all man that is born of a woman, has already the Ingredience or the seed of Fear in him because of Sin; which was made possible by the Disobedience of Adam and Eve in The Garden of Eden. Adam The Father of all mankind; realized the birth of a spirit that was unusual or unfamiliar; a spirit of Fear which came out of him the moment he disobeyed The Commands of God. This should make us to realize that every time we commit sin; that sin will birth a new spirit of Fear.

Genesis 3:10.

"And he said, I heard Thy Voice in the Garden, and I was **Afraid**, because I was naked; and I hid myself".

All our lives start from a foundation of a seed; whether it be the seed of sin or the seed of The Word of God; which then Develops to be THE TREE that we are effected to become; which then grows to bring forth the Fruits of that particular type of Tree. Fear caused by Sin will cause every Child of God, to hide themselves from The Presence of The Lord. But is hiding from God a wise thing to do? As if we can truly hide from God! The Lord Never Told us, that on this journey, we will never make a mistake; He Told us, that He have broken down the middle wall of separation that we can now have full access to come before God; Repent of our Sins; ask for Restoration; and He Promised that He Will Be There to Accept our prayers coming from A TRUE HEART.

To Overcome the spirit of Fear, a person have got to first acknowledge that the Fear does exist. This Fear is indeed a lack of Understanding and Knowledge; it therefore means that if we are Serving God and have not yet received or have Brought forth these Gifts of Understanding and Knowledge through The Holy Ghost that God Has Given to us; then we will always be that person which suffers from a spirit of Fear.

The Bible Said how can a man Cleanse his ways, but by taking heed to The Word of The Lord. Those of us that are reading this Message, for us to fully understand what Fear is; we have got to first Acknowledge that Fear is a Disease or an unclean spirit that have been allowed to grow in our lives, by the lack of our understanding of not being able to use The Word of God as a Guide, to ensure that we are Instructed and Lead in the right manner of how our life is to Operate.

The physical man suffers from all the evidence of the spirit of Fear; while the Spiritual man that is Born of God, shows absolutely no evidence of the spirit of Fear. The Bible Explains in The Book of St John 3:3.

"Verily, Verily, I say unto thee, Except a man be Born Again, he cannot see The Kingdom of God".

This The Lord Jesus Christ was Speaking to Nicodemus, explaining to him the DOOR in which he must travel in order to be SAVED; the Door that leads to a man not having any Fear of this present life; that Door is to be Born Again.

Examples of the Physical Man are seen in The Bible; which was Transformed or BORN AGAIN, to become A Spiritual Man of God. Peter although being chosen as the man that got the Revelation for knowing who The Son of man is; St Matthew 16:13-20. Peter in that state, was still in the physical life; because soon after that happen, he Feared what man would do unto him, if he had confess that he knew Jesus Christ. The Cock Crowed after he denied The Lord three times, manifesting to Peter and also to us, that Peter although was destined to be a Great Leader; at that time in his life, he was still A PHYSICAL MAN.

Example of A Spiritual Man. Stephen according to Act 7:55. Was a man being FULL OF THE HOLY GHOST; when they were throwing stones at Stephen for the main purpose that he should Die; because Stephen was now fully in The Spiritual Presence, verse 60 revealed that he said:

"Lord lay not this sin to their charge. And when he had said this he fell asleep".

Absolutely NO FEAR, because The Spirit of God Has No Fear. The Physical man, because there is an absent of The Word of God; that space that should be full with The Word, is now filled with the opposite of The Word of God, therefore allowing the Mind to be full of the directions or the paths of life it should now travel on which is vanity that brings forth Fear.

There is only two paths in this life:

Pathway or gate number (1). The Word of God which is Life and Truth; which brings Confident and Assurance to our spirit to know and to understand that God Already Fills The Universe, therefore there is absolutely no need to Fear.

Pathway or gate number (2). An absent or the lack of God's Word, which brings darkness, confusion, lack of confidence, a lack of faith; allows us to go down, and down a broad road of destruction; that it will appear that we are the person that will destroy our own life, because of a spirit called Fear.

The Bible Said that a man without God is Frustrated and Incomplete. We may ask why? This is the reason for it; God's Word has all The Ingredience to Full the Mind of a man, that he now will have The Ability or Power to become A Son Of God; it is the Mind that take control of the Body, allowing the body to Function as it should according to God's Word. The Word of God according to 1 Peter 1:13 Says:

"Wherefore gird up the loins of your mind, be sober, and hope to the end for the grace that is to be brought unto you at the Revelation of Jesus Christ".

The Mind of a man remains to be the most important part of that man; because whatever the Mind is fully Overcome by, that's what will Effectively lead that man in the pathway that he is to follow. If the Mind is Fixed in The Word of God, then there can be No Fear; therefore the whole body is healthy by the evidence of THE WORD OF GOD. If the Mind of a man is broken by Fear, then that man's life will be Fully overcomed by the spirit of Fear. We wonder why the Life of Jesus Christ had Great Effects to Change the whole direction of Mankind; Jesus Christ is The Mind of God in the Flesh in full effect; therefore He couldn't Fear because there is No Fear in God.

Question: Why should we Fear when that which is in us is Complete Understanding of All Things, both Physical and Spiritual; why Fear, when there is the Evidence of The Almighty Spirit of Knowledge; how could Jesus Christ Fear, when it is clear that He Is Wisdom; having Known about His death for centuries, before the Beginning of time, and also having the Understanding that His life will open the doors of hell for those who are kept captive; giving us His Believers the opportunity to now live above Sin and not in Sin; How could He Fear, knowing that He has All Power in Heaven and in Earth, to lay down His Life and then to Raise it up back again?

Again I say, Fear is an absence of Understanding, Knowledge and Wisdom of The Word of God; a disease or sickness that only affects the Minds of those who are Simple and Feeble; those whose Minds are not yet Trained to know what The Word of The Lord Says. Here is one thing of Confidence, that is said by The Word of God.

2 Timothy 1:7.

"For God Hath Not Given us the spirit of Fear; but of Power, and of Love, and of a Sound Mind".

Let us look at something Great. Isaiah 40:12-17. There is a part in this Scripture that Says:

"Who hath directed The Spirit of The Lord, or being His counsellor hath taught Him".

When we consider The Greatness of His Majesty, The True Power of His Might; should we be Fearing anything at all, now that we've become Sons of God? The answer is NO. Why Fear, when it is that our Father Says:

"All Nation before Him are as nothing; and they are counted to Him less than nothing, and vanity".

There is something of Fact, that I have discovered to be True, this is it; in all appearance that The Lord Presented Himself to His Servants in The Bible; there are two words that remains constant which says: **"FEAR NOT"**.

I would ask My Readers to Investigate for themselves, then we will realize that it is True. The main thing to look at is the word Fear Not, and not the word Fear by itself; therefore, if we are Serving God and is Traumatized by Fear; then The Gift that God Has Given us is not yet made Perfect, and is in need of work to become Perfect.

What is the Work? The Work is for us to Read to Understand about God. It is identified however that this path way of Faith is not the absence of Fear; but what The Lord Would Have us to realize is that if we but just keep our eyes Focused on Him; then we would have passed that which we Fear without realizing that we have passed that which we Feared. Fear is Real and is at a level, to make us Understand that to Trust God, far out measures the Level of Fear that is completely Overpower, and is Overcome by TRUST.

I made mention to the fact that Fear is Real and at a level; to allow us to Understand that as we live our lives for God, we are going to experience in our lives the evidence that we are going through and evolving to higher and higher levels; that when we have Reached to the Higher level than that of Fear, we will be Born to the Belief to now realize that although it is real, it now stands that it has no effect on our Walk with God; because our walk has now Elevated to a level of Complete Faith in God.

To Overcome Fear, is an Access Door that each Child of God has to first Find, in order to pass through, in order to Overcome that which we Fear. A Child of God however is not always willing to pass through that door, but would rather have to be forced to pass through that door.

Let's have a Look at some of the Doors of Fear that we are afraid to go through; of which we will discover that the more willing we are to attempt to go through these Doors; it will allow us no more to be afraid of these Doors; but we must remember that The Key to unlock these Doors, is The Word of God.

- ➤ A Fear to ask Questions.
- ➤ A Fear to say YES.
- ➤ A Fear to say NO.
- ➤ A Fear to give to God a full Surrender of our Life.
- ➤ A Fear to tell the Devil that we don't belong to him anymore.
- ➤ A Fear to admit that we are Afraid or when we are wrong.
- ➤ A Fear of Acknowledging who we truly are, but instead continue to Pretend.
- ➤ A Fear of seeking for True Love.
- ➤ A Fear to ask someone for Help.
- ➤ A Fear to be of Help to Someone in need.
- ➤ A Fear to sleep in our bed at nights.
- ➤ A Fear to stand up for what is Righteousness, to tell Someone what is wrong from what is right in The Eyes of God.
- ➤ A Fear to let people know that we are now SAVED.
- ➤ A Fear to speak the Truth, because it may cause us to lose our Jobs or a Friend.
- ➤ A Fear to Read The Bible.
- ➤ A Fear to come to Church; Fasting Service; Prayer Meetings; Sunday School.
- ➤ A Fear to Change from Darkness to LIGHT.
- ➤ A Fear to tell our friends about GOD, and invite them to Church.
- ➤ A Fear to be an Example; to become The Light of the World, A City set upon a hill that cannot be hid.
- ➤ A Fear to introduce our children to God; because if they get Saved, it means that we must remain Saved.
- ➤ A Fear to be alone, not knowing that it's when we are alone, that God Has Liberty to Commune and have Fellowship with us.

And these are only a few of the things we Fear.

Fear locks away the possibilities of Spiritual Maturity in God; which allows us to not be Trained, to be able See and to Understand that which God Needs us to Understand and know what we are Capable of doing only through God.

St Matthew 14:22-33. In this Scripture it explain that The Lord Jesus Christ Walked on the water to approach a Ship, that His Disciples were in; The Bible Said that Peter asked The Lord to Allow him to walk on the water to come to Him; this Permission was Granted, and he began to walk on the water, but when he lost Focused, on Whom he should be Focused on, The Bible Said that he began to sink; proving that he was not yet ready to Overcome that Door of Fear. The Lord Said to him:

"O thou of little Faith, wherefore didst thou Doubt?"

DOUBT brings forth FEAR; Doubt will prevent us from accessing any Door of Fear which we desire to walk through, in order to Overcome. Yes, we have to walk through that which we Fear, in order to Overcome that which we Fear.

Doubt Clouds our Mind, which shatters our confidence, and tell us that it is not possible; even when God Has Opened The Door for us to walk through it, in order to Overcome that Fear. Doubt prevents us from seeing The Light that God Needs us to see. Our number one enemy is Doubt which brings with it, the spirit of Fear.

2 Chronicles Chapter 20. In summary, The Bible Explains that there came many soldiers to battle the king of Judah; of which when he heard about the amount that came up against him, The Bible Said in verse 3 of this Chapter, that king Jehoshaphat Feared; but it didn't stop with a spirit of Fear; The Bible Also Said that while he Feared what was coming to destroy his people, he realized the most important ingredience, which was GOD.

The Bible Said that king Jehoshaphat set himself to Seek The Lord, and proclaimed a Fast throughout all Judah. The king, having A Relationship with God, realized that although the evidence was there for him to Fear; he knew that he Served A GOD that could pull down any door of Fear the enemy have put up. The Bible Explains that after he sought The Face of God, The Lord Gave them the assurance, that they wasn't even going to fight in this battle, because the battle is not theirs, it was The Lord's Battle.

Fact: Many times we Fear an obstacle in our path, that was only placed there for us to Know and to Understand that God Need us to Seek Him, so that He can Prove to us, that the battle is not ours to fight, but it's for Him to Fight. If we should be Truthful; how many times when something comes in our path way, that cause us to Fear; How many times do we approach God with the problem, and ask Him to Deliver us because no one else can?

Now we can understand why there is always a spirit of Fear in our Lives that refuse to go away; because we have not yet brought it to The Lord, by Seeking His Face for Him to Solve the problem for us. We desire to solve it on our own; not remembering that The Bible Said:

"Except The Lord Build the House, they labour in vain that built it". Psalms 127:1.

There is nothing that we can solve by ourselves, every step we make, it requires God's Guidance and Council.

I made mention at the beginning of this Message that The Lord Gave me A Vision concerning this Topic; I would like to share with My Readers this Vision. In My Vision I dreamt that I was at a place by myself; the dream felt familiar as if I had dreamt it before, but only now that I am in the Vision I discover that there was something familiar about the Vision. I dreamt I was by myself, then suddenly out of nowhere there came a little Bug, like the appearance of what we call a Grudgeful Bug; and this Bug was flying and pitching on me; and no matter how hard I tried to kill the Bug, by the time I violently attacked the Bug to ensure that he is dead, I realize that I missed the Bug. And I would try and try again to catch or to kill the Bug; but the faster I attempt to act, it's with the same speed that the Bug keeps avoiding my threats, and I didn't understand why.

It was then I realized that I had received A Vision like this in the past; an enemy that I could not destroy. The Lord Spoke to me in the Vision, and Told me that the reason I was not able to destroy or to catch the Bug, was because I was the person that gave life to that Bug; He Explained that the Bug was an insect that I did not like, therefore there was developed in the conscience of my Mind, a spirit of Fear towards that Bug. God Explain to me that I was the person that fueled the life of that Bug; therefore no matter how hard, and swift I attempt to catch or to kill that Bug; the Bug would still be able to evade my threats, because the Bug was Not Real, the Bug was just a spirit of Fear that I have developed in My Mind, therefore as long as that Fear for the Bug still exits, there will be nothing I could do to get rid of that Bug.

The Lord Was basically using the Bug to let me know that the more we add fuel to that which we Fear; it's the more it's going to seem Impossible for us to control; stop or kill that which we Fear. I was brought back to the Vision of the Bug, and then decided that I was no longer afraid of the Bug; then I realized that the Bug just disappear; no longer fast; no longer swift; no longer hard to kill; no longer a danger or threat to me; no longer in My Mind as a spirit of Fear; the Bug was no more because I stopped feeding that Fear.

I Thank God for Explaining to me The Vision in that order, that I can be able to know what is Fear. Fear is a Destructive spirit that seeks only to imprison the Minds of God's People; which if it is continued to fed, will result in the destruction of whoever it occupies.

My Belief after Receiving this Vision, is that 100% of what we actually Fear; is brought on by our Minds; thus we keep on feeding that which we Fear, we will end up being a vessel that only occupies Fear, instead of The Word of God. I know this Message was not only written for my benefit, but I believe that this Message will be an Inspiration to all those who read this Message. Remember, that which we fuel is what gives our Fear strength; No Fuel, results in No Fear.

All Praise goes to The God Who Is Alpha and Omega; The Beginning and The End; The First and The Last; Jesus Christ The Lamb Of God. From the Servant of God, Your Brother, Friend, Minister and Pastor Lerone Dinnall.

NO FEAR IN THE NAME OF JESUS CHRIST!

Focus

Message # 80

Date Started August 30, 2017
Date Finalized September 2, 2017.

1 Kings Chapter 13:7-10.

"And the king said unto the man of God, Come home with me, and refresh thyself, and I will give thee a reward. And the man of God said unto the king, If thou wilt give me half thine house, I will not go in with thee, neither will I eat bread nor drink water in this place: For so was it charged me by the Word of The Lord, saying, Eat no bread, nor drink water, nor turn again by the same way that thou camest. So he went another way, and returned not by the same way that he came to Bethel".

Greetings in The Mighty Name of Jesus Christ Our Soon Coming King, The Saviour of Mankind. Again let me offer all The Praise to God which Liveth Forever and ever. It is Ironic to come to the Understanding that after we've read this Passage of Scripture, it bears a sense of witness to suggest that here is a person that have come to the realization to know what it takes for someone to become and to Maintain A Spirit to be Focused. Then it is realized after reading the complete Chapter of 1 Kings Chapter 13. We then discover that this story resembles the entire lifeline of human history according to Bible Teachings; that being Man's ineffectiveness to follow through on that which God Has Asked us to carry out. A Complete Unreliable Body of Flesh we have found ourselves to occupy.

The Bible Made Mention that flesh is so unreliable, that the Best state that a man may accomplished, in God's Eye, it is less than nothing. It is also made mention in The Book of Romans 7. Brother Paul sharing his experience about the Carnal man, in comparison to that of The Spiritual Man in one Body. Verse 14-25 Says:

"For we know that the law is spiritual: but I am carnal, sold under sin. For that which I do I allow not: for what I would, that do I not; but what I hate, that do I. If then I do that which I would not, I consent unto the law that it is good. Now then it is no more I that do it, but sin that dwelleth in me. For I know that in me (that is, in my flesh), dwelleth no good thing: for to will is present with me; but how to perform that which is good I find not. For the good that I would I do not: but the evil which I would not, that I do. Now if I do that I would not, it is no more I that do it, but sin that dwelleth in me. I find then a law, that, when I would do good, evil is present with me. For I delight in the law of God after the inward man: But I see another law in my members, warring against the law of my mind, and bringing me into captivity to the law of sin which is in my members. O wretched man that I am! Who shall deliver me from the body of this death? I Thank God through Jesus Christ our Lord. So then with the mind I myself serve The Law of God; but with the flesh the law of sin".

We may wonder why it is that a person who has been overwhelmed by the spirit of Pride; that person in God's Eye has acquired a status of becoming an ABOMINATION. The reason for this is because, when man has moved his desires from The Only Living God, to now have full confidence in his own Abilities; of which those abilities in God's Eye are to be compared to Vanity, which only last for a Time, then after the Time and the Season have been completed, the abilities of man are no more. And when man's time and abilities are now dead, there will still be The Living Almighty God.

There is one main thing to Understand from the passage of Scripture in 1 Kings Chapter 13. That being that the enemy will never give up on trying to allow God's People to lose their Focus.

After the Young Prophet was successful to overcome the Temptation of the king's offer, The Bible went on to say that there was also an Old Prophet in the same country, that persuaded the Young Prophet by telling him that The Lord Sent him to tell him that he no longer needed to carry out The Strict Instructions, but that he should go home with the Old Prophet, Eat and Drink. The rest of the story explained what happen; but what I need My Readers to Understand, which is going to be Mind Blowing, is that it wasn't a Sinner that came to the Young Prophet! It was a man like himself that was in the Lineage to hear from God and to carryout God's Direct Instructions.

This story is very touching; I'm sorry for what happened to the Young Prophet, but I'm happy for the example of Life Training. We could just imagine that the Young Prophet had his Guard Up when it came to be in the Environments and Atmosphere of Sinners; and then being happy that he has overcome the Atmosphere of Sinners to now be in the Atmosphere of a fellow Brother and Sister, this gives a sense of peace, or so he assumed. One of the clear examples of how to maintain being Focused is to make certain that we as Children of God are 100% Focused in the Environments of Sinners, and at the same time to make sure that we have Elevated to a Level of 200% Focused in the Environments of those who we esteem to be our Fellow Brothers and Sisters in The Lord. I know that this is hard to swallow, but The Bible is there for our Example, to Teach us what happened in the past, so that we can make a brighter future, by preventing the same mistakes to be repeated within our lives.

There is one thing that we need to Understand, and that is, not everyone we see in The Church or going to Church are completely Born Again; Rather it is always the few in number, The Tithes of Saints that are really Born Again; those who are walking after Holiness. We are most of the times around Mixed Multitude, and majority of that multitude has a Crab in a Barrel Mentality; meaning, if God is not going to Use them to do something, then God Shouldn't Use anyone else; that was the type of spirit the Old Prophet had. And we as True Children of God need to be very careful of those who we are comfortable around, because those people will allow us to lose our Focus. And many times it is not the Mind Frame for those around our Circle to be obstacle that cause us to lose Focus, but Rather they are found to be needing of that Special Anointing Touch, which will also see them rising to The Level of Spirituality to also maintain a Discipline to remain Focus, that no one will cause another to Stumble because of a Lack of Focus.

St Matthew Chapter 14:25-33.

"And in the fourth watch of the night Jesus went unto them, walking on the sea. And when the disciples saw him walking on the sea, they were troubled, saying, it is a spirit; and they cried out for fear. But straightway Jesus spake unto them, saying, Be of good cheer; it is I; be not afraid. And Peter answered him and said, Lord, if it be thou, bid me come unto thee on the water. And he said, Come. And when Peter was come down out of the ship, he walked on the water, to go to Jesus.

But when he saw the wind boisterous, he was afraid; and beginning to sink, he cried, saying, Lord, save me. And immediately Jesus Stretched Forth His Hand, and Caught him, and said unto him, O thou of little faith, wherefore didst thou doubt? And when they were come into the ship, the wind ceased. Then they that were in the ship came and worshipped him, saying, of a truth thou art The Son of God".

While it is observed that A Child of God desires to remain Focused, we must remember that this Discipline to be Focused has got to be Tried and Tested, thus Manifesting to ourselves and to God that we are an Available Vessel that can be used to Fulfill God's Work.

Note: Those who are used to Manifest for God successfully, are those who have perfected the Discipline of what it means to be Spiritually Focused. Now according to the Webster's Dictionary, the word Focus Means:

"A Central Point, as of Attraction, Attention, or Activity".

The word Focus explain, that there must be A Focus Point; and to ensure that such a person has completely acquired and Mastered The Discipline and The Spirit of God to be Focus; such an individual has to be Tried and Tested, Burned according to The Level of Heat that The Lord Will Allow, just to ensure that, that which God Has Allowed to Bear in us, is of The Right Fruit.

To Understand being Focused at the point that the Test is being administered, The Lord Reveals that the Wind and the Waves of such a person Focus, are indeed the Forces and Adversaries that have been Released for one purpose and one purpose only, that being to ensure that those who are walking in The Spirit to acquire the things and The Blessings of The Spiritual are indeed those who have been given the Access by God through the Foundation of His Word Remaining in that Individual's Life.

The Lord Reveals that a person without the Infilling of The Holy Ghost cannot be Spiritually Focus; therefore such a person can never Walk in The Spirit to Acquire The Spiritual Blessings and Favors that The Lord Has in Store for The Sons of God.

There is A Natural Focus, and there is A Spiritual Focus. Whenever The Holy Ghost has brought forth The Fruit of The Spirit of Focus in a Believers life, because that Believer has grown in The Word of God and The Manifestation of God's Action. Then such a Believer will immediately recognize the Big Difference from Natural Focus to that of Spiritual Focus.

The Lord Reveals that such privilege are so precious, that only a few being The Tithes of the Saints are given the Access to Walk in The Spirit by Seeing what The Spiritual has to Offer. Those who Walk in The Spirit by Seeing The Spiritual are not easily shaken nor are they Afraid of anything because The Foundation of God's Word would have found Root in that person's life, to now become The Only Solid Rock. The Adversaries that are sent and are released to try the Focus of a Believer, there main job is to become the Biggest Distraction in that Believer's life. Meaning that, that which we would have put most of our Value on, it is that very item or things that the spirits of distractions are coming to interfere with and use as a major distraction to allow that believer to take their eyes off The Focus Point.

"You've Been warned"!

Now The Focus Point is always The Promises that The Lord Has Planted within the Life of a Believer. Therefore it is important for My Readers to Understand that we must always seek to write down all that God Has Promised that He Is Going to Fulfill within our lives; by doing this, it acts as A Spiritual Fuel for when the spirits of the Adversaries is Released, and it is now felt; then such a Believer in order to remain in The Spiritual Focus, that believer can go back to The Words which The Lord Has Spoken over their Lives, to thus overcome the passing Challenges that seeks to kick us back to the Natural Focus.

The Adversaries are the spiritual Gates and Doors, that a Believer must be able to use The Spiritual Key to unlock those Doors and Gates; and that Spiritual Key is one, that being The Undiluted Engrafted Word of God The Almighty. The Undiluted Engrafted Word of God is The Revelation of The Word that we read in The Bible. Many people are confident that they know The Word of God by reading through The Bible; which is good and has its merits, but how many of us have been given the Privilege to know THE GOD HEAD, to Understand What The Word is Saying and How it must be used in our personal life; and that's the big difference from Natural Viewing to that of Spiritual Viewing.

When the Distraction Arise, just remember to say what God Has Promised you; the Higher the Distraction, Just say God Says_____ and God Says_____ and God Says_____ Amen and Amen so let it Be What God Has Said.

Doubt is the number one enemy of The Spirit of Focus. And if there is found in a Believer's life the spirit of Doubt, that means that The Spirit of God has not yet been Perfected within the life of that Child of God. Because it is a Fact, whenever time A Child of God is now Full of The Word, Full of The Revelation of God; then there can be no spirit of Doubt to hinder the life of A Child of God.

I remembered having a conversation with God when I just got Saved; I was praying to God and explaining that I was terrified to be in the Dark; meaning I could not sleep in the dark, there had to be some night light; I could not walk in the Dark; if I reached a point on the road that was very dark, I would run through that area just to prevent from walking in the dark. When I mentioned this in My Prayers to God; The Lord Spoke to me and Said:

"The reason why you're so Afraid of the Dark, is because there is a Lack of My Words in you, My Word is Light; therefore if you have My Word in you, you will no longer be afraid of the Dark".

When I got that response, I realized that I needed to start A New Diet, that being to ensure that I begin to know The Word of God for myself. To God Be The Glory, I'm no more afraid of the Dark.

A Child of God have got to Learn how to prepare themselves before they even walk out the door; especially if we are called to perform a specific Duty for God; we must remember that we are Soldiers in God's Army, therefore we have to be Strategic in everything that we do in this World because the World is always viewing that which we do, and then to compare our lives to what The Word of God Says, so that they can now find reasons to judge. Also the World knows everything that we have done yesterday, therefore to make a plan for us for Tomorrow is very easy. And that's where The Spirit of God comes in; because we are patterned to do what is expected of us to do; there will at times be Traps and Snares waiting to Tangle our feet and hands to the will and direction of the World.

A Child of God has got to Understand that there are Gateways to the Soul, and the Soul is the most important thing that each person has. And if we are not careful to protect these Gateway for our Soul, then we will be corrupted by the Influence of the World. The World has become very wise, because of the master that governs it; therefore, The Children of God has got to become Double if not Triple the abilities of the World. And the only way we can do that, is not to compete with the World, but to compete with ourselves to challenge ourselves to know more about God's Word. Because God's Word Has in it the Ingredience of Revelation, that which the World can never and will never come to Understand, because it is Spiritually Discern for those who are Spiritually Focused.

A Child of God Must Guard that which they allow themselves to See, we are not privileged to see everything, because there are some things if we see them, it will bring forth a Permanent Crack in our Vessels. We must Guard against that which we Smell; there are some Colognes that have in it the Ingredience, the Recipe that will Trigger the Sexual hormones of those who have smelled of that fragrance. Then we wonder how is it that our children start to behave in a particular manner after we have allowed them the access to encounter with different groups. And not only to Trigger our Sexual hormones, but also to Trigger a spirit of Fear and Anxiety within the life of A Believer. Some things that we Smell allows us to become very Angry, wanting to curse whoever we see; and because we are not knowledgeable of the Device and Practices of the World, we are often time fallen into the Traps and Snares of the Enemy, because we just do not know what the World is Doing, we are in a state of IGNORANCE.

We must Guard against that which we Eat and Drink from whosoever we Eat and Drink from, if it is possible, we must try to consume that which we have prepared for ourselves, if not, then we must make sure that we Bless and Eat. There are Substance that are sold in Pharmacies, that if it is placed within the drink of an individual, the reaction from that person that have drank will result in complete loss of Self-control. I told especially the Sisters that are of My Assembly, to make sure that whatever they are Drinking or Eating, to make sure that they are the person that have first opened that container, whether it be Food or Drink; and also to make certain that if for any reason they have to leave the container of that which they are eating and drinking, they must be discipline enough to make sure that they don't return to continue that meal or drink.

"IT IS A WARNING"!

We must Guard our Soul against that which we Feel, meaning Touch and Handle things with our Hands, especially Money, and those money that are coming from people who seek the practices of Divinations, those Money that instead it allow us to be Build, it causes us to be Cut down; we must use The Gifts of The Holy Ghost to Discern who it is that we should take Money from; and what we should do when those Money come in our surroundings. Remember that the number one job of The Holy Ghost is to Protect The Temple of God. We must be careful of those whose hands we shake, it is the Practices of Diviner to allow spirits to be transferred by just a Touch, and by just a Touch A Child of God Anointing can be quenched, meaning become weak; because we have touched that which require A Higher Level of God's Anointing for us to be an Overcomer; if we are not sure of the persons hand we are shaking, then refrain from shaking hands; this is not to say that God Cannot Allow an Individual to reach a Level that these things doesn't affect them, but until that time has Arrived, The Children of God has to be extremely Careful, especially in these times; because the enemy has now realized that we are no longer Fools concerning his Devices, therefore the enemy is seeking for other ways and through other mediums through which he can now disguise himself to fall into the lives of God's Chosen People, to the effect that he will destroy God's Inheritance. Truth, if we are not in the Future able to fulfill The Purposes of God, then it is a Fact, we are Destroyed from doing God's Purpose.

We Must make certain to Guard ourselves concerning those who desire to put their hands in our Head; especially if that hand is not Anointed to fulfill that purpose of Blessing. Those who by joke or jester that comes around us to rub their hands in our Heads, they know what they are doing! It's only because we are STUPID why we have not realized as yet what they are doing to us. It is a Practice of Divination, that they have used certain Substance to rub in their hands, then to Rub their hands in our Heads that we will be confused, that the outcome will be that they will Control Us.

The Mind Control the Body; therefore, those who have the spiritual influence by means of Divination are those who have God's People on a string like a Puppet. I cannot emphasize enough how Dangerous Laying On of Hands Truly is. You go to Church, and everybody is picking up the Practice that they want to Lay Hands on God's People; it has now become a Job, that they look forward to be doing; because they know that by doing what they are doing with the Practice of Divination, that they can continue to suck The People of God dry of their Anointing that God Has Bestowed upon that Individual's life.

For The Priest, The Bishop or The Pastor, it is not a problem for those persons to Pray for us, because they are God's Anointed. Therefore when they Pray, The Anointing and Favors of God will be Released or Should be Released, if it is that such A Priest; Pastor or Bishop is Anointed by God. And if they commit themselves to such Practices of Divination; then don't worry because God is our SURE REWARDER.

A Child of God must consider their Head to be Off Limits for all those who are not an Anointed Vessel of God. You've Been Warned! A Child of God must be certain of the Foundation of whosoever they come in contact with. Light can never be Darkness, neither can Darkness be Light. There is a saying that goes like this:

"God Call Fools, But He Doesn't Keep Them; Because when He Calls Them, He Is Expecting those Persons to Become Wise Through His Words".

There is a Famous saying from The Man of God, Bishop Austin Whitfield, and I Quote:

"You Can't Throw Powder On Black Bird, Because After A While That Bird Is Going To Shake The Powder Off, And Return To Being What Was His Origin".

This is in no way a racism comment, because I asked him what it meant; and he told me that there are many that will come to God for Salvation, but it is only those who have Fully Repented, will experience the Transformation of Christianity; others that have not Repented will only remain to be what they were before they came to God, no matter how much we Pray and Fast for those people, they will just remain to be the same. So I got the full Understanding coming from the mouth of The Late Bishop Austin Whitfield.

Becoming Wiser in God must now be the Motto of God's People. The enemy does not like us, doesn't like our Children and our Husband and our Wives, and it is a certain he will never in the future be able to tolerate us; therefore Children of God, the Name of the Game Is:

"The Wise Children will Survive; The Foolish Children will become like the Five Foolish Virgins".

We must Guard our Souls against that which we Hear, we should not be hasty to hear everything, especially those things that are coming from those who are not Saved. If a person's Foundation is Darkness, what can they really tell you, that will enable The Light of God to become Brighter in your Life. A Consecrated Child of God is A Separated Child of God, which means that we are Set Apart for only God's Use. The Children of God Must Guard our Souls concerning where we go, some places are Amusement for the Altar of the Devil, and because it is Covered or Disguised; without The Spiritual Focused Eyes we will not be able to Understand that we are on the Altar of Idols, offering the sacrifice that strengthen that Idol.

Serious Times Children of God, these are Serious Times, therefore the Times require Serious Service for God and also Serious Christians. If you don't have to smile don't smile, because a smile can be interpreted in many different ways. The days are upon us that The Lord Says:

"Watch therefore: for ye know not what hour your Lord doth come". St Matthew Chapter 24:42.

We must Guard against those who have access to come in our Homes; I have felt the damage of this practice first hand. And it is a lesson that I need not to learn again. We must Guard against those who have be given access to drive with us in our Cars; YES, let everyone make their assumptions of what they think about your Practices or Disciplines; if Adam had it to do all over again, he would make sure that he never leave the side of Eve, and also to ensure that she makes no Decisions! That's the danger of time, once it has past, it can never be retained. We would now have to live with the Consequences of the Mistakes we have made in the past.

I've had My Experience of carrying Church members in my personal vehicle, and afterward discover substance with strange smell in the very vehicle that I'm driving. Therefore, what I'm saying to My Readers is not something that is made up, or what I think, but rather what I've experienced. It's Time to get Sharpen People of God, It's Time to Become Focused and Remain Focused. We Must Guard ourselves concerning what we wear, as in clothing; different type of clothing entertains different type of spirits.

Just have a look around, and you will discover that the World with all its Leaders, Kings, Queen and Prime Ministers and Presidents, they are completely Confused, which is the opposite of being Focused; and if they are not Focused, then we need to ask the Question: Where can they Lead us? But in a Dark Bottomless Hole! The Call of The Lord is upon us which Says:

"Seek ye The Lord while He may be found, call ye upon Him while He is near: let the wicked forsake his way, and the unrighteous man his thoughts: and let him return unto The Lord, and He Will have mercy upon him; and to our God, for He Will abundantly pardon". Isaiah Chapter 55:6&7.

We have even discovered that the Money that everyone is killing themselves for, that very Money have now become of No Value! And very soon The Bible Will Be Fulfilled which sees Money on the Ground, and no one having the Desire to even pick it up, because of the plagues that shall be Released upon the Land.

FOR SAINTS

For those My Readers that have received a copy of this Message; Use and Take this Message has a Wake Up Call. Get Ready, Be Focused; Read more and more of The Bible; do more Prayers; go to more Fasting Services and Sunday or Saturday School and Bible Classes, thus to ensure that we are filling our Vessels with enough of God's Anointing, and remember that your Anointing is yours, not to be shared with those who are Foolish, but to be kept safely for The Calling of The Bridegroom. Be Ready Waiting, it's a Warning!

FOR THE UNSAVED

For those who are not yet Saved, if it is that you have found yourself reading this Message, count yourself has being Privileged and Blessed, that God Has Chosen you to Know what is to Come, and what is happening now around you, and RUN FOR YOUR LIFE. Free Will; your Freedom to choose. If it is that you're considering about your SOUL, that's Good. You have to choose for yourself, and become determined to make a Change, because Change is coming, whether or not you're ready for that Change. Find A Church that has The Revelation of Jesus Christ Being God, Repent of your Sin, which means to Turn, to Change from what you were doing, to that which God now Need you to Do. Get Baptize, Seek to Receive The Gift of The

Holy Ghost, find a seat in Zion and make sure you Learn about God, because Time Clock is Striking the Hour, The Trumpet of The Lord will soon be Sound. Make sure that you are a part of The Saints when we are Being Caught Up Into Glory.

You've Been Warned!

To The Only Living God, Jesus Christ The Lamb of God, to Him Be All The Glory, Honor and Praise. From your Friend and Company in this Life, Pastor Lerone Dinnall.

Remain Focused On God.

To Declare And To Decree; With Knowing That It's Not Just Coming From The Mouth.

Message # 4   Done in the year 2015.

Praise Jesus Christ Saints of God; I am happy to be writing for you a next Message which was Inspired by God. I must say that I Give God All The Glory, The Honour and The Praise for this privilege that He Has Afforded me to write unto His People; I say thank you Lord.

Above is a Topic that may be a little unusual to many but let me say that it is necessary for God's People to know about this Message. To Declare and to Decree this sounds easy, many may say; but is it easy to do, or to make happen? That's the question that we would like to find out.

The first time I looked on this Topic, when The Lord Gave it to me for Study; I speak the truth, I felt a little Nervous; why you may ask? When I look at the meaning of the words, I got to realize that these are words that are Associated with God Himself, especially the word that is called Decree.

Now at all times, we as Children of God have got to be careful that we are never in a position that we take God's Glory for ourselves; and especially those responsibilities that Belongs to God. But when I went further in My Studies, I got to realize that God Is Already God, and at all times through all Generations and Dispensation, God Has His People that He Uses to Represent God on Earth. And one of the Functions that God Equips His Servants with, is the Ability to Declare and to Decree what is in The Mind of God. Think about it, if God Did Not Equip His Servant with this Ability, how would we know, what God's Instruction Are.

To Declare and to Decree, what does this Mean?

Does it mean that I can use this Gift for my own selfish desire and wishes?

The Answer is NO.

Just look for a minute what it means; to Declare and Decree means that we get the Opportunity to become God's Mouth Piece, to speak what is in The Mind of God. It therefore means that we will only be Used, according to The Direction to which God Needs us to be Used. If we are not speaking what Says The Lord, then any other words, will have no Power or Effect.

Here is a question that we can ask ourselves, how do we become A Servant that will be Used to Declare and to Decree What God Says?

The first thing we need to know is that we must be Filled with The Holy Ghost. The next thing is that we must be Filled with The Word of God, meaning, we must know The Word of God, in order to Understand What The Words Mean.

The next thing to know is that it must be Imparted upon our lives by God Himself. It is God that Does the Choosing, He Know who will be A Good Servant; from him that will be A Bad Servant.

I know we must be asking ourselves this Question: What is the difference between being Filled with The Holy Ghost and being Filled with The Word of God?

Let me say this, I have seen many People or Saints receive The Holy Ghost and because they do not Sustain or Feed The Holy Ghost it becomes Dormant in their lives. The job for all Saints when we Receive The Holy Ghost is to make sure that we are also Filled with The Word of God, thus ensuring that we do not leave any space in our lives for the devil to creep back in. The whole Bible is filled with persons who

God Has Inspired to be His Mouth Piece; for them to Declare and to Decree what is in The Mind of God.

Exodus 3. Speaks about Moses; Numbers Chapters 22 and 23. Speaks of a Prophet called Balaam, that was instructed by Balak King of Moab to curse The Children of Israel, but because The Children of Israel was God's Chosen People whom God Blessed, and Balaam was an Instrument Used by God, he could not do or say something that God Did Not Order him to say or do, even though he was promised a lot of riches and up to half of a Kingdom. Joshua was also called to be A Servant of God, and he was Given The Instructions that he needed to carry out, in order to Remain God's Instrument. Joshua 1:1-9. And there are many others.

Let's break down this Topic a little bit that we can understand it better; to Declare means to make known; to state clearly; to announce officially. This word is a verb, which means that it takes action to accomplish this task. The word Decree means a formal order having the force of law; "This word is one of The Eternal Purpose of God". This word can either be used as a verb or a noun.

Now this is the statement that gets me Interested; why; you may ask? The Lord Would Have me to realize that The Word of God Is Decreed, and brought into action when it is known by the individual and also used, therefore allowing it to be a verb. On the other hand Decreed as a noun is explained, meaning The Word of God Remains in The Bible by us The Children of God, and is never used, because we don't see the importance of reading The Word of God to Empower ourselves, therefore The Decreed Word of God Remains a noun because it is in a Book.

Another way it was Revealed being a noun, is when we as Children of God do read The Word of God, but never bring it into action, therefore it remains something inside of us that is never used; a Noun Decree. How do we Declare and Decree? Think about it; do we speak, and whatsoever we speak, think or believe it will be done? Or is it that I've Matured in God and know about God and His Word; and His Word have now become a part of me, that when I speak through

The Leading and Direction of God, I know that it is done. The second option sounds a lot more like the answer.

The Power to Declare and to Decree is found in The Word of God. Yes, that statement is 100% True. Think about it and observe, that same Bible that many of us Misuse and Mistreat, Abuse and also Abandon, it is that Bible that has The Decreed Word of God. The same Bible Gives us Instructions that we must Search The Scriptures; for in them ye think ye have Eternal Life. St John 5:39. It also said that man shall not live by bread only, but by every word that proceedeth out of The Mouth of The Lord doth man live. Deuteronomy 8:1-3. What is The Word that proceedeth out of The Mouth of The Lord? It is The Bible that we forsake; but yet we need life and The Power to Declare and to Decree; without The Word of God, this will never work.

Why do we need The Word of God in us to Declare and to Decree, you may ask? When we ask a request from God, not many People or Saints know that God First, Searches our Minds and our Hearts to See if we are Abiding in Him; now if when He Searches, He Finds The Word of God in us, then He Will Recognize us as being A Son of God, and therefore Sees it as His Responsibility to Answer our Request that we have asked for according to His Will. If He does not Find His Word in us, then He Has no Obligation to Answer our Request, though we may cry for long Hours, many Days, Weeks and Months, and even Years, and do so with many Tears. St John 15:1-16. And not only to read The Word of God, but also to do exactly what it asked for us to do; because it is not the Hearer or Readers are Justified, but those that Do what The Word of God Asked them to Do. James 1:21-27. To Declare and to Decree only comes through Obeying The Word of The Lord.

In this Message that we are reading, I have a home work for us to research for ourselves: Read The Book of Joshua Chapter 1, from Verse 1-9. And after we have read this passage, I need us to ask ourselves this Question; Would God Fulfill His Promises to Joshua, if Joshua decided that he was not going to Follow The Commandments of God? I leave My Readers to Answer that Question, _____.

So is it with many of us, that when God Makes us a Promise we may think that God Promises does not come with Conditions Applied.

Learn this, and the sooner we learn it, it will be better for us; God and His Words Are One, it therefore means that whatever God Promise or Declare over our lives, it must be in Direct Connection with His Word, and the Requirement for us always, is for us to Do What His Words Command us to Do.

Failure to Do God's Word, will result in a breaking of The COVENANT that God Has Made between God and His People. Therefore, Don't expect God to Give us anything, because we are not going to get it, if it is that we are outside of God's Will. In Deuteronomy Chapter 28. Please ensure that we read this complete Chapter in order to understand what The Word is saying over our lives.

In The Book of 1 Kings 18:21-40. It speaks of a comparison between two (2) set of people, one set of people were numbered four hundred and fifty (450). The other set was just one man by the name of Elijah who had The Anointing and True Power of God over his life. The first set was given a challenge to call on their gods to burn a Sacrifice, of which they prayed, they cried, they cut themselves, and do harm to their bodies, but there was no god to answer them. This prayer was done for almost a full day, but there was no god to answer them.

Elijah being one man, but one man with a Difference, prepared his Sacrifice and made sure that he made it extremely difficult for the Sacrifice to burn, Elijah Prayed unto The God of Abraham, Isaac and Israel, and Immediately God Acknowledge the Prayer of Elijah and sent fire from Heaven that Devoured the Sacrifice that Elijah made so difficult to burn. This story is given to us that we can Identify for ourselves The Power that God Has Invested in One Man; and that one man can be anyone of God's People Today; if we decide that we are not only going to Read The Word of God, but also to Know to Understand that we are Able to Do The Word.

And this is what God is Waiting on from you and me to make us Great, that we may have The Power like Elijah to Declare and to Decree. Every time we fail to do what is right according to The Word of God, it brings forth Limitations in our own Vessels and Restrict us from doing what we should actually be doing in God, which is to Declare and to Decree. God Need us to Learn how to be like Him, because to be like Him is the only Acceptable way to make it into Heaven.

To Declare and to Decree is an Accepted Spirit of God in us, which God Has Identified that we are not only Filled with The Holy Ghost but we are Now Full of The Holy Ghost, and His Word is being Manifested in us by our Deeds; therefore allowing us to become The True and Complete Spirit and Likeness of God.

I Give God All The Glory, The Honour and Praise. To My Church Family and all other Saints of God, I say thank you for Reading this Message I hope it was A Blessing to our lives and also, that it will bring forth changes in our lives. From The Servant of God, and The Ministry of The Church of Jesus Christ Fellowship Savannah Cross Ltd. God Blessing Always, Pastor Lerone Dinnall.

To Declare And To Decree;
With Knowing That It Is Not Just Coming From The Mouth, But From The Spirit Man.

Closing Scriptures

2 Chronicles Chapter 29:16-19.

And The Priests went into the inner part of The House of The Lord, to cleanse it, and brought out all the uncleanness that they found in The Temple of The Lord into The Court of The House of The Lord. And The Levites took it, to carry it out abroad into the brook Kidron. Now they began on the first day of the first month to Sanctify, and on the eighth day of the month came they to the Porch of The Lord: so they Sanctified The House of The Lord in eight days; and in the sixteenth day of the first month they made an end. Then they went in to Hezekiah the king, and said, We have Cleansed all The House of The Lord, and The Altar of burnt Offering, with all the Vessels thereof, and The Shewbread Table, with all The Vessels thereof. Moreover all The Vessels, which king Ahaz in his reign did cast away in his transgression, have we Prepared and Sanctified, and, behold, they are before The Altar of The Lord.

Nehemiah Chapter 12:27-30.

And at the Dedication of the Wall of Jerusalem they sought the Levites out of all their places, to bring them to Jerusalem, to keep the Dedication with gladness, both with Thanksgivings, and with Singing, with Cymbals, Psalteries, and with Harps. And the sons of the singers gathered themselves together, both out of the plain country round about Jerusalem, and from the villages of Netophathi; Also from the house of Gilgal, and out of the fields of Geba and Azmaveth: for the singers had builded them villages round about Jerusalem. And The Priests and The Levites Purified themselves, and Purified the People, and the Gates, and the Wall.

Conclusion

I Thank You Heavenly Father, In The Name of Jesus Christ that You
Have Allowed this Book to reach The Minds and Hearts of Your People,
I Thank You for Allowing me to be A Vessel Available for Your Glory.
I Thank You for the Lives that this Book will Change; I Thank You
for those that will have a Firmer Grip on Their walk with You; Lord I
Thank You that Your Will Is Being Done on Earth has it is In Heaven.
In The Name of Jesus Christ, I Say Thanks.

I've Learnt from one of My Instructors while attending A Training
Seminar, that if a person learn what is being Instructed, it would mean
that the Attitude of that person have also been curved to Learn what
is being Taught. My Encouragement for all those who have Read this
Book, make certain that the words of this Book Transforms our Souls
to Change, and if we are already Changed, ensure that these words
allow for us to Elevate to The Continual Higher Level In God. We owe
it to ourselves to ensure that we do everything within our Power, we
must make certain that we spend our lives knowing about The Will
and Commandments of The Most High God.

After we've successfully Rebuilded our Spiritual Wall through
The Help of Almighty God, It is My Prayer that we will Become
Wise to A Touch, to thus ensure that we do everything that we can
do to Keep those Walls as High as they can be, and also to hold firm
The Teachings of God that we never forget, that when God Blessed
us, He Did Not Forget About Our Generation, therefore Disciplined

Teachers we Must Become, to fulfill The Mandate of God that we can continue to Train Our Children in The Will and Requirements of The Almighty God.

Deuteronomy Chapter 30:15-20.

"See, I have set before thee this day life and good, and death and evil; In that I command thee this day to love The Lord thy God, to walk in His Ways, and to keep His Commandments and His Statutes and His Judgements, that thou mayest live and multiply: and The Lord thy God Shall Bless thee in the land whither thou goest to possess it. But if thine heart turn away, so that thou wilt not hear, but shalt be drawn away, and worship other gods, and serve them; I denounce unto you this day, that ye shall surely perish, and that ye shall not prolong your days upon the land, whither thou passest over Jordan to go to possess it. I call Heaven and Earth to record this day against you, that I have set before you life and death, Blessing and cursing: therefore choose life, that both thou and thy seed may live: That thou mayest love The Lord Thy God, and that thou mayest cleave unto Him: for He Is thy life, and The Length of thy days: that thou mayest dwell in the land which The Lord Sware unto thy fathers, to Abraham, to Isacc, and to Jacob, to Give Them".

To The Only Unlimited Mind of The Universe, Jesus Christ, To Him Be All Honor, Glory and Power. From The Ministry of The Church of Jesus Christ Fellowship Savannah Cross Ltd. Jamaica West Indies, GOD'S BLESSING ALWAYS, IN THE NAME OF JESUS CHRIST.

Printed in the United States
By Bookmasters